Stephen Chambers

Everyday Life
in the
Roman Empire

Family dinner, Arlon

Everyday Life

in the

ROMAN EMPIRE

JOAN LIVERSIDGE

Drawings by Eva Wilson

B. T. BATSFORD LTD
LONDON

G. P. PUTNAM'S SONS
NEW YORK

First published 1976
Text © Joan Liversidge 1976
Drawings © B. T. Batsford Ltd 1976

ISBN 0 7134 3239 X
LCC NO. 76–13350
American SBN: TR 399–20554–3
                    BG 399–61043–X

Filmset by Keyspools Limited, Golborne, Lancashire
Printed and bound in Great Britain by
Butler & Tanner Ltd, Frome, Somerset
for the Publishers
B. T. BATSFORD LTD
4 Fitzhardinge Street, London W1H 0AH

G. P. PUTNAM'S SONS
200 Madison Avenue, New York, NY 10016

CONTENTS

7

8

9

THE ILLUSTRATIONS

ACKNOWLEDGMENTS

The Author and Publishers thank the following for their kind permission to reproduce copyright illustrations. The Publishers apologise if they have unwittingly omitted to acknowledge any sources or made any incorrect attributions.

Frontispiece Musée Archéologique, Metz

1, 2 Musée d'Aquitaine, Bordeaux

3 Benn, London: G. Bean, *Turkey's Southern Shore*, 1968

4 Verlag Franz Deutcke, Vienna: F. Miltner, *Ephesos*, 1958

5–7, 9 Historische und Antiquarische Gesellschaft zu Basel: R. Laur-Belart, *Augusta Raurica*, 1959

8 Historisches Museum, Basel

10 Stiftung Pro Augusta Raurica, Basel: *Das Römerhaus in Augst*, 1956

11, 12 E. Schulz, Basel/Stiftung Pro Augusta Raurica, Basel

13 Rheinisches Landesmuseum, Bonn

14 Fayard, Lyons: A. Audin, *Lyon : Miroir de Rome dans les Gaules*, 1965

15, 16 Société Anonyme de l'Imprimerie A. Rey, Lyons

17, 18 Rheinisches Landesmuseum, Trier

19, 20 American School of Classical Studies, Athens: *A Brief History and Guide*, 1968

21, 22 Weidenfeld & Nicolson, London: V. Caffarelli and R. Bandinelli, *The Buried City*, 1961

23 Musée de Châtillon-sur-Seine

24, 25 Musée d'Aquitaine, Bordeaux

26 Institut Archéologique, Arlon

29 Musée Archéologique, Dijon

30 Musée Lapidaire d'Arles/H. Roger Viollet, Paris

31 Greven Verlag, Cologne: O. Doppelfeld, *Dionysiac Mosaic near Cologne Cathedral*

32 Bodley Head, London: J. Balsdon, *Life and Leisure in Ancient Rome*, 1969

33 British School in Rome: *Papers*, 1948

34 Department of Antiquities of Tripolitania, Tripoli: D. Haynes, *Antiquities of Tripolitania*

35 Fayard, Lyons: A. Audin, Lyon: *Miroir de Rome dans les Gaules*, 1965

36 A. F. Kersting, London

38 Editora Stiintifica, Bucharest: D. Tudor, *Oraşe Tîrguri şi sate în Dacia Romană*, 1968

39 Musée Archéologique, Metz

40 Musée Archéologique, Dijon

42 Musée Gaumais, Buzenol/Clém. Dessart

43 Rohrer Verlag, Vienna: A. Schober, *Die Römerzeit in Österreich*, 1954

44 Musée d'Aquitaine, Bordeaux

45 The Clarendon Press, Oxford: C. Singer et al., *A History of Technology*, vol. 2, 1956

48 British School of Archaeology in Iraq, London: *Iraq*, vol. 11, 1949

49 Imprimerie Nationale, Paris: E. Esperandieu, *Repertoire des Bas-Reliefs Gallo-Romaines*, vol. 4, no. 2769, 1911

52 Thames & Hudson, London: K. D. White, *Roman Farming*, 1970

54 The Clarendon Press, Oxford: M. Rostovtzeff, *The Social and Economic History of the Roman Empire*, vol. 1, 2nd edn., 1957

55 Altertumsmuseum und Gemäldegalerie, Mainz

56 J-L. Combes, Tunis

57 British School in Rome: *Papers*, 1953

58 Thames & Hudson, London: K. D. White, *Roman Farming*, 1970

59 Rheinisches Landesmuseum, Trier

60 The Clarendon Press, Oxford: M. Rostovtzeff, *The Social and Economic History of the Roman Empire*, vol. 1, 2nd edn., 1957

61 Comitato de la Documentazione dell' Opera dell' Italia in Africa, Rome: S. Aurigemma, *Italia in Africa. Tripolitania I. I Monumenti d'Arte Decorative*, Pt. 2

62 Editions du Centre National de la Recherche Scientifique, Paris: G. Fouet, *La Villa Gallo-Romaine de Montmaurin*, 1969

64 Kölnisches Stadtmuseum, Rheinisches Bildarchiv, Cologne

65 The Clarendon Press, Oxford: C. Singer et al., *A History of Technology*, vol. 2, 1956

66 Weidenfeld & Nicolson, London: V. W. Von Hagen, *Roads that Led to Rome*, 1967

67 Römisch–Germanischen Zentralmuseum, Mainz
68 Rheinisches Landesmuseum, Trier
69 Bell, London: R. Wiseman, *Roman Spain*, 1956
70 Econ Verlag, Dusseldorf: R. Portner, *Mit dem Fahrstuhl in die Römerzeit*, 1960
71 Service Nationale des Fouilles, Brussels
72 British Museum, London
73 The Clarendon Press, Oxford: M. Rostovtzeff, *The Social and Economic History of the Roman Empire*, vol. 1, 2nd edn., 1957
74 Altertumsmuseum und Gemäldegalerie, Mainz
75 Mansell Collection
76 Rijksmuseum van Oudheden, Leiden
77 Department of Antiquities of Tripolitania, Tripoli: D. Haynes, *Antiquities of Tripolitania*
78 The Clarendon Press, Oxford: M. Rostovtzeff, *The Social and Economic History of the Roman Empire*, vol. 1, 2nd edn., 1957
83 Musées Archéologiques, Nîmes
84 A. F. Kersting, London
85 Musée Départmentale des Vosges, Epinal
87 Plon, Paris: H-P. Eydoux, *La France antique*, 1962
86, 88–90, 93 Rheinisches Landesmuseum, Bonn
92 Verlag Gebr. Mann, Berlin: E. Gose, *Der Tempelbezirk des Lenus Mars in Trier*, 1955
95 Bureau de Tourisme et d'Information de Turquie, Paris
96 Conseil National du Tourisme au Liban
97 Chatto & Windus, London: M. J. Vermaseren, *Mithras, the Secret God*, 1963
98 C. Buchners Verlag, Bamberg: *Germania Romana*, vol. 4, 1928
99 Verlag der Löwe, Cologne: F. Fremersdorf, *Der Römergrab in Weiden*, 1957
100 Benn, London: G. Bean, *Turkey's Southern Shore*, 1968
101, 102 ACL, Brussels
103 Rheinisches Landesmuseum, Trier
104 Department of Antiquities of Tripolitania, Tripoli: D. Haynes, *Antiquities of Tripolitania*
105 Conseil National du Tourisme au Liban

I

Introduction

Many books have been written about the Roman Empire and to attempt to present within the confines of a single volume a picture of the daily life of its inhabitants seemed at the outset a task calculated to arouse serious misgivings in all but the most foolhardy scholar. The area concerned is vast, stretching as it did from Scotland to North Africa, all round the Mediterranean shores and on into Romania, Turkey and Syria. In it lived people of very diverse backgrounds who had attained varying degrees of civilization. Different circumstances of conquest or alliance brought them into the Empire so that Rome, its government and institutions, was often the only link between them.

Much evidence for the everyday occupations of the Empire's inhabitants comes from contemporary art, literature and inscriptions. Still more has been found by the archaeologists working on ancient sites in all the provinces, and it is the enticing nature of some of this material which has inspired the present work. Ideally one would wish to survey life in each province and consider the relationships between them, how they influenced each other as well as how far provincial influences affected Rome, for the traffic in ideas did not emanate only from Italy. In practice it has merely proved feasible to pick out certain topics rather arbitrarily, guided by the interest of the evidence available. While it seemed advisable to give some account of towns, no detailed discussion of architecture or, alas, art, could be included. Religion, too, has had to be confined to some account of pagan beliefs. In any case these subjects are well covered by other authors.

No historical survey has been attempted but a chronological list of emperors will be found in Appendix 1. In general this book discusses the Empire in the late first and second centuries A.D.,

SARMATIA

MARE CASPIUM

ACIA

ESIA

DANUVIUS

PONTUS EUXINUS

CAUCASUS

THRACIA

ARMENIA

DONIA

Byzantium

BITHYNIA et PONTUS

ASIA

GALATIA

CAPPADOCIA

ASSYRIA

CHAIA

Athenae

Ephesus

LYCIA et PAMPHYLIA

CILICIA

MESOPOTAMIA

Antiochia

Palmyra

CYPRUS

SYRIA

CRETE

Tyrus

JUDAEA

ene

Alexandria

Petra

ARABIA

NAICA

AEGYPTUS

before the invasions of the third century began a period of insecurity and economic stress. Material from every province has been used but Egypt and Britain receive little attention. The former because the evidence, although abundant from this country with its ancient civilization, tends to apply particularly to Egypt and not necessarily to other provinces. The latter because there are already so many publications concerned with Roman Britain readily available to English-speaking readers.

Two topographical problems arise. In using place-names it has seemed best to adopt the most familiar. Some ancient names are now unknown while other sites, such as African desert towns, have Latin names but no easily recognizable modern equivalents. So Paris and Lyons occur and so do Lepcis Magna and Volubilis. As far as possible all names are noted in the index with the ancient or modern alternatives, present country and Roman province. The other problem is the relationship between the Roman Empire and modern geography which is sometimes difficult to discover. As the map on pages 20–1 can only be on a small scale, a list of the provinces giving their approximate location when this differs substantially from the modern equivalents, is also included (Appendix 2).

I am indebted to many friends for help and information, in particular to Miss Joyce Reynolds for reading the manuscript although she is in no way responsible for the result; to Miss Pamela Lloyd and Mrs Sylvia Christiansen for typing the manuscript and assisting with the index; and to Mrs Eva Wilson for her drawing of the line illustrations and the map on pages 20–1. The dedication to Dr Nora Kershaw Chadwick is a small thank offering to a much-loved friend who inspired so many scholars with her lively appreciation of the continuing importance and interest of the past.

JOAN LIVERSIDGE, 1976

2

The development of towns

The diverse elements which were incorporated into the Roman Empire are well reflected in the development of town life. Before discussing this important topic, however, it is advisable to consider to what extent people were living in towns before the Roman conquests. In Greece, Egypt and the eastern Mediterranean countries, for example, there was already an ancient tradition of urban civilization which had blossomed into the splendid Hellenistic cities of the third and second centuries B.C. As a result, in these areas, the majority of the towns are of pre-Roman origin, and the Roman contribution chiefly consists of a few new buildings or the reconstruction of old ones.

Along the coast of North Africa, pre-Roman developments have also to be taken into account. In Egypt the ancient civilization of the Pharoahs was overlaid by the work of the Hellenistic dynasty of the Ptolemies, and Cyrenaica has also produced evidence of strong Ptolemaic influence. Further west comes the area previously under Punic (Carthaginian) rule, and across the Mediterranean this also applies to the southern coastal areas of Portugal and Spain. In southern France, Greek colonization initiated urban settlements at a number of sites including Marseilles and St Rémy.

PRE-ROMAN SETTLEMENTS
The situation before the Roman conquests in the rest of France, Britain, the Low Countries, the Rhineland and the frontier provinces along the Danube, is less clear. Numerous tribes controlled these territories, and their lands varied in extent according to the success of their inhabitants in waging war on their neighbours, making successful tribal alliances, or profiting from trading opportunities. In these circumstances the less warlike tribes tended to be driven out of the more fertile areas

into marshy or hilly country. However the growing up of a fresh generation of young warriors or the appearance of a new leader with either diplomatic or martial ability could soon change the fortunes of an individual tribe.

Most of these tribes practised agriculture and stock-rearing in varying degrees. Among them were skilled craftsmen including smiths who used the more easily accessible mineral resources to make weapons, and also luxury objects of great beauty such as horse trappings, armour, jewellery, or mirrors for the chieftains and their families. Their living conditions, however, were simple, usually timber-framed huts with walls of wattle and daub, sometimes small individual farms or else several huts grouped haphazardly without much attempt at planning.

The chieftains, on the other hand, tended to live with their retainers in the larger fortified settlements which the Romans called *oppida*, frequently placed on hilltops or in some other defensible position. In times of war the rest of their followers with their families and animals might also take refuge there. These settlements were often encircled by formidable ramparts and ditches, and the construction of such defences must have required planning and organization. Among the huts inside it is sometimes possible to identify the home of the chieftain. It may be larger, stand a little apart, or, on excavated sites, prove to be the one hut to contain weapons or jewellery. An example of this is the fine spearhead from the chieftain's hut in the Iron Age hill fort on Hod Hill (Dorset) which can be contrasted with the piles of slingstones which is all the excavation of other huts produced.

Primitive as most pre-Roman settlements seem, there are exceptions such as the *oppida* encountered by Caesar in central France, the great *oppidum* on the Danube at Manching near Ingolstadt, or the settlements developing in England just prior to the Roman invasion of A.D. 43. One such was Camulodunum (Colchester, Essex), chief city of the powerful Belgic tribes and well-placed for continental trade up the river Colne. Defended by a series of dykes, the site does not seem to have been intensively occupied; perhaps space was left for refugees in emergencies. Whether such sites would have developed into towns if they had lacked the spur of Roman occupation is a debatable point.

This is the kind of background upon which were to be superimposed the characteristic types of Roman town. To the provincials the arrival of many of the complexities of the

Imperial administration must have seemed quite bewildering, and none more so than the appearance of officials sent to build a settlement to a pre-arranged plan with roads, public buildings and water supplies. Simple thatched huts would be replaced by timber or masonry houses with tiled roofs; the collection of all the building materials alone would be a major undertaking.

EARLY ROMAN TOWNS

In newly-conquered territories the first cities to appear were known as *coloniae* or colonies. They were built and inhabited by soldiers recently discharged from the army. On retirement each man was entitled to a plot of land as a gratuity, and the skills learnt on active service would be used to organize the erection of houses and public buildings. The emperor would give each colony a charter laying down its constitution with its name, rights and privileges. The latter usually included freedom from the taxes levied on other provincial communities, while the governor, who ruled each province as the emperor's lieutenant, could normally interfere little with the colony's affairs.

The administration of the colonies closely copied that of Rome. A senate or town council, the *ordo*, elected two chief magistrates known as the *duovirs*. They acted as mayors and justices of the peace, and were assisted by two *aediles* who were primarily responsible for roads, market dues and water supplies. City treasurers, known as *quaestors*, might also be appointed. Such appointments, the election procedures, the spending of public money, and many other aspects of city affairs were meticulously laid down in the charter. The colonies acted as models for the development of other towns, and their inhabitants demonstrated the Roman way of life to the provincials and so spread Romanization. In some areas, where unrest still existed, the veterans could also act as a military reserve.

Cities which were already in existence in newly-acquired areas might also be given a charter and absorbed into the Empire with the title of *municipium*. These charters were inscribed on sheets of bronze and set up for all to read. Copies were also kept in Rome. Fragments of first-century charters conferred on Salpensa and Malaca in Spain by the Emperor Vespasian still survive, and show a system of local government very similar to that of a colony. In some cases, however, a new *municipium* which already had a council and magistrates could choose to continue its traditional way of life, subject to Roman approval. The charters were varied to suit individual circumstances.

All these chartered cities had a certain area of land attached to them for cultivation. Its rents boosted city finances while the produce helped to feed the inhabitants. The rest of the land was divided into areas which frequently coincided with the territory inhabited by a particular tribe. With the end of tribal warfare and the building of roads, the larger native settlements grew gradually into towns, often with less organized planning than we find in the colonies and *municipia*. The administration of the less civilized areas was at first a military responsibility which was later handed over to a civilian official known as a procurator, until the new towns grew sufficiently to be entrusted with their own affairs. Their local government would develop on the Roman pattern but on a smaller scale, beginning with only two magistrates, often descendants of the chieftains or other tribal aristocrats. These varying types of civilian administration gave great flexibility.

The townsfolk took a great pride in their cities, and as the cities grew the emperor would receive petitions asking for a charter. This might be conferred as a special favour or in recognition of increased importance and development. So Claudius recognized the support of the people of Volubilis in Morocco in wartime by the grant of the status of *municipium* (see p. 67). After a time colonies ceased to be founded exclusively by veteran soldiers, and we know from a third-century inscription at York that a large settlement, which had grown up outside the legionary fortress there, had successfully applied for a colonial charter. In fact the status and prestige of the colony grew steadily as such cities were felt to be the closest provincial equivalent to Rome itself. The Roman Empire looked on the provincials as friends and allies rather than subject peoples, and as a result Roman ways were adopted with enthusiasm in many of the provinces.

ROMAN CITIZENSHIP

The veteran legionaries who built the first colonies were already Roman citizens. For other people citizenship was obtained in various ways. We know from the references to St Paul (*Acts* Chapters xvi and xxii) that this was a much coveted status, carrying with it social advantages which made it very attractive to ambitious men.

The chief privileges of the citizen included *commercium*, the right to carry on personal business affairs according to Roman Law. Roman laws were very comprehensive, regulating many of the details of daily life as well as major legal issues, and courts with qualified judges were usually available. For merchants in particular, trading perhaps in several different provinces, this ability to conduct business transactions always under the same conditions was a great benefit. The other major privilege reflects the intense interest felt by the Romans and by those influenced by them in the making of wills. This was *conubium*, the ability to make a marriage recognized by Roman Law which safeguarded the legitimacy of the children and their rights of inheritance. Other forms of marriage existed but were not legally valid. Citizens in trouble were also less liable to suffer torture and other summary treatment in case of arrest.

Apart from inheriting citizenship from citizen parents, there were various ways of obtaining this coveted status. Non-citizen soldiers received it when they completed their service, and could then legalize their marriages and pass on citizenship rights to their children. Local magistrates and town councillors often obtained it as a privilege of office. Tradesmen in particular were keen to acquire the right of *commercium*, and there were many individual grants of citizenship for various reasons. It has been estimated that retired auxiliaries alone would add about 5,000 new names to the register every year, so the number of citizens soon grew. Sometimes, as in the case of Volubilis, the status was conferred by an emperor on a whole city. Finally in A.D. 212 the Emperor Caracalla conferred the citizenship upon almost all the free inhabitants of the Empire.

Besides Roman citizenship, it was also customary for individuals to have local citizenship, a privilege confined to the people of each particular town which could be granted to resident aliens—often traders.

Local affairs were left in the hands of local people under the general oversight of the governor of each province as far as possible, so long as law and order were maintained and the magistrates produced the taxes for which they were responsible. Tribal law continued in use for non-Roman citizens, and the emperor's legal experts who assisted the governors in some provinces may have attempted to reconcile Roman and native laws when problems arose.

Every five years the chief magistrates checked the register of members of the *ordo*. Usually there were 100 town councillors, known as decurions. They had to be local citizens who had homes within a radius of a mile of the city centre, free-born men of substance and mature years. There is some doubt as to the minimum age limit, although in certain places 22 or 25 is attested. The property qualification was probably 100,000 sesterces. Occasionally, in towns where local circumstances justified it and it was difficult to find sufficient suitable men to complete the *ordo*, freedmen, who had started life as slaves but had gained their freedom and prospered, were admitted, and also the occasional resident alien. New decurions paid a heavy initiation fee for an honour which also entitled them to special seats in the theatre and amphitheatre, and exemption from certain forms of punishment if they fell foul of the law. Normally election was for life.

THE TOWN COUNCILLORS

Much of our knowledge of local administration including the work of the *ordo* comes from the charters of the *municipia* of Salpensa and Malaca, and the colony at Urso (Osuna) also in Spain, which was founded by Julius Caesar in 44 B.C. We learn that a quorum of two-thirds of the members of the *ordo* had to be present to audit accounts, decide to build new aqueducts, or to declare certain dates as days of festival. Half the *ordo* could authorize the dispatch of embassies or the demolition of buildings (anyone destroying a building without permission was liable to a very heavy fine unless he rebuilt it within a year). Fifty decurions had also to be present for decisions concerning public funds, buildings, open spaces and roads, while forty were needed to permit citizens to use excess water from the reservoirs for baths or dye works. Twenty could authorize payment for the contractors who provided the wine, animals and sacrifices for special occasions.

The Urso charter reminds us that no one could be nominated as a magistrate who was not eligible for election as a decurion. A would-be magistrate must be free-born, solvent, of good reputation and with no court convictions. The charters include warnings against influencing voters with presents or entertainments before elections. After election, however, a substantial donation to the town was expected from a successful candidate.

According to the Salpensa charter the magistrates had to be sworn in at a public meeting five days after their election. They swore by Jupiter, the deified emperors, the genius of the current ruler, and the city's gods to rule in the common interests of the citizens in accordance with the charter. Anyone neglecting to take this oath could be fined 10,000 sesterces. The citizens were grouped in voting wards and during elections the votes were placed in ballot boxes. Each ward had its own separate voting booth supervised by three citizens from different wards who counted the votes and drew up a list of results. If two candidates tied, the married man with the most children headed the list and his name went forward.

SLAVERY

Besides the dignitaries on the council and the other citizens, a town's inhabitants might include free men who had not attained citizenship, traders and other aliens whose homes were elsewhere. The manumitted slaves, known as freedmen, had citizen status if they had been freed by Roman citizens, although they were still affected by certain restrictions. There may also have been slaves still in bondage.

It is difficult to assess the part played by slavery in the ancient world, and in modern times the subject is somewhat charged with emotion. While slavery formed an integral part of the Roman way of life, it is doubtful to what extent it was adopted in the provinces. Inscriptions provide us with a few examples and there are occasional literary references to gangs of slave farmworkers or miners. Slaves were often prisoners of war, either as a result of Roman conquests or the victims of intertribal warfare who had been sold by the victors to slave-dealers. Occasionally a bankrupt individual would sell himself to pay his debts. As time went on most slaves were the children of slave parents.

Slaves were acquired by purchase or inheritance and were the absolute property of their master. They had no legal rights, and life for those working in gangs in the mines or on large estates must have been arduous and unhappy. On the other hand some slaves might be esteemed members of the household. Slave children were sometimes brought up with their master's children, their future masters, and might even share part of their education. From the mid-first century there was an increasing tendency to treat slaves more humanely, encouraged by the fact that as wars became less frequent, they grew scarcer and more expensive; but cases of extreme cruelty still occurred. Most slaves were employed as secretaries, doctors, stewards, butlers, cooks, valets, lady's-maids, hairdressers or craftsmen. In a large household, a slave might rise to a position of importance. Some lived to a ripe old age: one slave couple at Carthage were 102 and 80 respectively when they died.

Sometimes tombstones testify to the affection between master and slave. Thus at Bordeaux there is a monument erected to the memory of the 18-year-old Cintugnatus, slave of Publius Lucius, which was decorated with a portrait bust of the deceased (*1*), this monument was erected by Lucius's son. Found with it was the tombstone of another slave, Martinus, erected by his brother Crescens, the slave of Flavinius (*2*). At Tarragona in Spain there is a memorial to 'the most faithful slave' Augustalis, and the tombstones of Nicias, aged 30, and Optatus, aged 40, both slaves of C. Memmius Gallus, have been found at Sabora. Nicias is remembered by his mother and sister, and for both the wish is added, 'may the earth be light on thee'.

1   The slave, Cintugnatus, Bordeaux   *2   The slave, Martinus, Bordeaux*

Memorials show that slaves could accumulate some money of their own from gifts or from business activities promoted by their masters. In time they might save enough to buy their freedom. Others were freed by their master's kindness, often through instructions contained in his will. The new freedman took his old master's name as his own family name and continued to perform certain services for him and look to him for help and protection. Sometimes he continued as a member of the household, sometimes he would be helped to establish himself in some other occupation. Freedmen frequently dedicated altars for their patrons' welfare. At Bath (Aquae Sulis) Aufidius Eutuches and Aufidius Lemnus both did this to the goddess Sulis in honour of the centurion M. Aufidius Maximus. Officers on active service seem sometimes to have depended upon their freedmen for adequate burial, and Favonius Facilis owes the first-century tombstone which still survives at Colchester to Verecundus and Novicius, slaves whom he had freed. In Spain Masclia Glauca, a freedwoman and heiress, remembered her patroness Masclia Augusta; and a patron Salvius Bathillus, put up a memorial altar for a well-deserving freedwoman. Another Spanish tombstone was erected to C. Julius Gallus by Julia Prima, wife and freedwoman, to her husband and patron; here we may suspect a romance.

TOWN PLANNING

Some description of towns of various types from all over the Empire, selected to illustrate characteristic buildings, shops and private houses will be found in Chapter 3. Any student of Roman provincial architecture cannot fail to be impressed by the colossal amount of building which went on, and to wonder how it was all organized. When the decision was taken to build a new city on a site where there was no earlier settlement, an official and a team of land surveyors were appointed to direct the work. These surveyors, called *grommatici*, were skilled professionals who formed a special branch of the imperial civil service. Besides actual town-planning, their work included the allocation of land for cultivation outside the city limits, and also the detailed surveys of property and agricultural land needed for taxation purposes. The army had its own surveyors and these, too, were sometimes loaned to assist in town planning.

Once the site had been chosen, the city limits were marked out and sacrifices were made to the gods. The typical Roman town was a rectangle bisected by two main roads which crossed at right angles in the centre. Then the rest of the area was divided into a neat grid of numbered blocks called *insulae*, separated by side-streets. This arrangement is well-illustrated by the plan of Augst (5). The chief public buildings were sited near the centre of the town. They included the forum, the main town square, an open space surrounded on two or three sides by shops and offices with colonnades in front of them. In the centre of the square stalls were put up on market days. The inhabitants met in the forum to shop and exchange news. In bad weather the colonnades provided shelter and advertisements or election notices were often scribbled on the columns. Across the fourth end of the forum was the basilica, an aisled building big enough to hold large assemblies. At each end there might be a raised dais where the city magistrates presided over their courts. A council chamber for the *ordo* often led out of the basilica (6).

At least one set of baths would be built, probably more. Roman baths resembled Turkish baths with rooms of increasing temperature warmed by hypocausts. For this typical system of heating, a Roman invention, currents of hot air from furnaces were directed beneath raised floors which were supported on short pillars of tiles, and up tile flues built into the walls. The floors of the heated rooms grew so hot that thick-soled sandals had to be worn by the bathers. Once the building was heated, it was easy to maintain a constant temperature. Few town-houses had private bath-suites and, as a daily bath was customary, the public baths acted as a social club. They were open at different times for men or women, at a small charge. Often an open space, the *palaestra*, was provided for games and exercise. Refreshments were obtainable, and gambling was a favourite pastime. Other public buildings such as theatres and temples are discussed in Chapters 4 and 8.

WATER SUPPLIES

The importance of the baths emphasizes the fact that one major need of a city was a good water supply, as wells or rivers could not always produce enough fresh water for a town of any size. A city which could afford to build an aqueduct would employ a trained surveyor, probably an officer lent from the nearest military unit.

One of the magistrates would then put the building contract out to tender; the contractor deposited money as a guarantee that he would carry out the work. The land needed for the construction was bought by the city and, as there was no law of compulsory purchase, this could be expensive. Sometimes, as happened at Vienne, a local benefactor would pay for some of it.

The surveyor marked out the aqueduct's course with the help of the *dioptra*, an instrument used with levelling rods which could measure horizontal angles like a theodolite, or the *chorobates*, a large plank about six metres long supported on legs and adjusted with plumb-lines or a water level. Water from the source was collected in a basin and then travelled through stone-built channels or stone, earthenware, or lead pipes. Mountain springs were preferred as the water was usually moved by gravitational flow. Only a slight slope was needed but to maintain this, diversions sometimes had to be made round hills and valleys, or the aqueduct might be carried across low ground on arches. Other hills were traversed by tunnelling, a more expensive solution, the tunnels being dug from shafts excavated along the line (these shafts continued in use as man-holes for maintenance purposes).

Roman engineers were aware of the principle that water will find its own level and some stretches are built down steep slopes and up the other side. At the bottom of the slope the pressure of water and air in the channels was considerable and there was a serious risk of burst pipes, so the water flowed into a collecting chamber and was sent on its way up the hill through a series of small lead pipes or siphons, while ventilation allowed the air to escape.

On reaching the city the aqueduct fed more tanks or *castella*, often placed near the city walls. Then the water was distributed by low pressure to the fountains, public baths and official buildings. The surplus might be used by private householders, and the overflow from the fountains was also available for industrial purposes, flushing drains, etc.

One of the finest examples of a Roman aqueduct may be seen at Aspendus in Pamphylia. The water from mountain springs crossed the marshy plain through a stone water-channel carried on arches, the arcade also carrying a road (*3*). The stretch illustrated shows it approaching from the background to a point where the water ascended into a tower 30m. (97½ft) high,

3   The aqueduct, Aspendus

changed course, and descended again. Above the tower was an
unroofed basin accessible for cleaning by a staircase. Here surplus
air could escape from the channel and the extra height
maintained the pressure. Tiberius Claudius Italicus donated two
million denarii to pay for this water supply.

Sometimes mistakes occurred, as when Nonius Datus, a
surveyor from the Third Legion stationed at Lambaesis, planned
the aqueduct for Bougie (Saldae) in Algeria. His plan completed,
he saw the work started and returned to his unit. A letter of A.D.
152 from the procurator to the governor of Numidia relates the
sequel: at one point the aqueduct had to be tunnelled through a
mountain; when this point was reached after four years' work,
two parties of workmen began to dig from each side but somehow
they missed each other. Nonius Datus was urgently recalled.
After an adventurous journey involving a skirmish with brigands
he arrived and went with the procurator to the mountain. There
he found that his specifications were quite correct but that the
contractor had failed to follow them. Detachments of marines
and auxiliaries were sent for and the work completed. The letter,
quoting Datus's account in the first person, was inscribed on a
pedestal at Lambaesis.

PUBLIC BENEFACTIONS

The emperors financed many public buildings and the provision of aqueducts was one of their favourite benefactions. Ephesus, for example, owed the Aqua Julia to Augustus. Hadrian was one of the most generous benefactors. He visited more cities than any other emperor and the writer Dio Cassius mentions his gifts of water supplies, public buildings, harbours, money and various honours to many of them. In Africa, the colony of Lepcis Magna, birthplace of the Emperor Septimius Severus, owed to his patronage the splendid third-century forum and basilica; and the colonnaded street leading down to the harbour was considerably expanded during his reign.

Imperial help might also be forthcoming in time of trouble. In A.D. 64 the city of Lyons (Lugdunum) sent a donation of four million sesterces to Nero for the rebuilding of Rome after the great fire. When Lyons itself suffered a similar disaster a year later, Nero sent a contribution. Asiatic cities affected by earthquakes also benefited from imperial generosity, and in 26 B.C. Augustus helped to rebuild the gymnasium and other buildings at Tralles. Famines also aroused imperial concern and Domitian was quick to send officials to relieve a local scarcity at Antioch in Pisidia.

There was fierce rivalry between towns for the possession of splendid structures. Rich men had few outlets for their wealth. They could use it to buy property or else to make gifts of public buildings, thus ensuring that their names would be remembered as donors. Usually they were further commemorated by their fellow townsfolk with a statue or other memorial. The nature of such gifts was varied. Large contributions to the town treasury were not uncommon. Aponius Cherea, a mid-second century *quaestor* of Narbonne, gave his city one-and-a-half million sesterces, and Bordeaux once received a gift of two million.

In A.D. 19 Caius Julius Rufus erected a monumental gate at the approach to the Roman bridge over the river Charente at Saintes, dedicating it to the Emperor Tiberius and his son and adopted son Drusus and Germanicus. Rufus traced his genealogy back to his great-grandfather Epotsorovidius, chief of the local tribe, the Santones, through his grandfather C. Julius Gedemo, who became a Roman citizen, and his father C. Julius Otuaneunus. Increasing Romanization is shown by the disappearance of the Celtic names. He was also the high priest of the cult of Rome and

Augustus at Lyons and gave that city its amphitheatre in honour of the same emperor.

In Spain C. Valerius Valerianus, a magistrate and high priest at Torre de Zambra (Cisimbrium), fitted out the forum and built a temple with statues of five deities accompanied by five statues of himself. Money was left for poor children at Seville (Hispalis), and under a will, the citizens of Barcelona were left money invested at five per cent to celebrate the testator's birthday.

Excavations have also revealed some homely details about public buildings in the province of Dalmatia. Originally in the roughly built forum at Delminium both the basilica and the council chamber had entrances from the courtyard which had no colonnades. These entrances faced north and the *ordo* soon found its council chamber too draughty. The doorway was blocked up, a new entrance was made through the basilica, and a fireplace installed. Further inland at the rising town of Domavia, perhaps for the same reason, the double doors of the heated rooms in the public baths were hinged to the wall at an angle to ensure that one door at least was always shut. And in the dressing-room of the women's baths, 33 cloak pegs survived, still attached to the wall.

At the great port of Ephesus the street running up from the harbour still preserves its late fourth century paving; and an inscription records that in this area there were 50 lamps; this is rare evidence for street lighting but it was also known at Antioch. The gateway to the market or commercial area was a gift made by two wealthy freedmen in 3 B.C. Many years later, in the third century, an inscription was put up there praising a market official for keeping down the price of bread to four obols (about 3p) for a 14-ounce loaf. Another gift was the gymnasium of Publius Vedius Antoninus of A.D. 150, a building which combined the Roman baths with a Hellenistic type of gymnasium, a place for artistic and educational activities as well as a training centre for athletes (*4*). Vedius dedicated it to the goddess Artemis and his friend the Emperor Antoninus Pius. He also built the odeum and repaired the theatre. Apparently he had some difficulty in meeting the costs; when appeals to his fellow-townsmen failed, he applied to Antoninus Pius. The Emperor came to his rescue and also rebuked the Ephesians for their meanness, commending Vedius's public spirit compared with citizens who bought popularity with games or distribution of money.

Public buildings once erected had to be maintained and so gifts

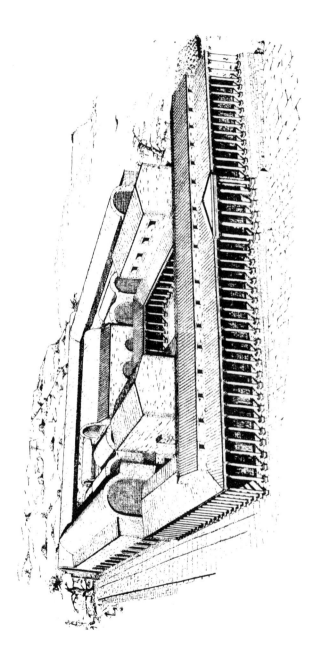

4　*The gymnasium, Ephesus*

became increasingly concerned with restoration and improvement. M. Ulpius Carminius and his wife gave 105,000 denarii for public works at Aphrodisias, and this fund was used for seats for the theatre, renovations to the forum and porticos, and interior fittings for the basilica, pillars and other decorations. They also gave money for distribution to councillors and townsfolk, a gift which has many parallels elsewhere. Another couple, Aurelius Jason and his wife Julia Paula, donated a records office to the same city, and this involved renovating older colonnades, many shops, and a library.

FINANCE

Apart from such gifts town revenues were chiefly obtained from rents for land in the territory around the town, which often increased in extent as the result of gifts and legacies, and from other natural resources. Fines, water-rates, the small charge for the use of the baths, market taxes and sometimes local customs duties contributed smaller amounts. An inscription from Ephesus lists some of the charges payable to the city council; they include licence fees of one denarius for sellers of salt and parsley, or for registration of a birth, while six denarii were payable for a proclamation announcing a victor at the games.

Rivalry in erecting fine buildings led some cities to overspend, and gradually the central government began to supervise their expenditure more closely. The correspondence between Pliny, when governor of Bithynia, and the Emperor Trajan illustrates the types of problem which arose. The city of Nicomedia had spent 3,318,000 sesterces on starting an aqueduct which was later abandoned and demolished, while more money was wasted on another failure. For such a large and prosperous city a water-supply was essential, so Pliny ordered a survey to find suitable springs. He then suggested fresh building using the old masonry or bricks which would be cheaper. Trajan approved, but instructed his governor to find out who was responsible for the previous waste of money.

At Nicaea ten million sesterces had been spent on a half-finished theatre on a damp site. The foundations looked none too solid to Pliny and the building was sinking and cracking. A new gymnasium to replace one destroyed by fire was also badly planned and an architect, admittedly a rival of the one who planned it, declared the walls were unlikely to be strong enough to support the superstructure. This time Trajan left the decisions to Pliny, remarking how the Greeks loved a gymnasium but adding that they must be content with one which was within their means. A reminder to see that private gifts of colonnades etc. promised for the theatre materialized is included in this letter.

In some cases the governor's inspection of municipal accounts enabled profits to be reclaimed from building contractors. At Prusa an ambitious building plan intended to provide 'tall buildings worthy of a great city, in place of low and mean ruins', met with such opposition that the promised gifts were withheld and little was accomplished. The townsfolk then petitioned for new baths to replace a dilapidated building; Pliny decided that these were necessary and could be financed by calling in individual loans and using money usually spent on distributing free oil to the bathers. It may have been Trajan who began the custom of appointing imperial agents to supervise town expenditure, one official sometimes dealing with several towns.

3

Examples of towns

We have seen how the new Roman cities developed great pride in local citizenship and competent administration, and how such amenities as public buildings and water supplies were provided and financed. Let us now look at how some typical towns of varying importance grew up in the different provinces. They include the colonies at Augst, a city built in newly conquered territory; and Lyons, a great commercial centre; a small flourishing town at Vaison; a military market town at Heddernheim; and Aquincum, a Danubian colony developing from a settlement of traders attracted by the nearby military fortress. In the Eastern Empire, Corinth, and in North Africa, Lepcis Magna and Volubilis also follow earlier settlements. These are all sites which can be visited and where in most cases, some of the buildings survive.

AUGST

Many of the typical features of Roman town-planning can be seen at Augusta Raurica or Augst, near Basle, Switzerland. It was founded on 21 June 44 B.C., three months after the death of Julius Caesar, by one of his lieutenants, L. Munatius Plancus. Built on the upper Rhine and near the frontier, it was a city created for the settlement of veteran legionaries who, by making their homes there, would set an example of Roman urban life to the neighbouring tribes(5). Enough survives to show that the site was laid out in the usual neat grid pattern, but in the north-west corner this careful planning was upset, possibly to avoid some earlier religious sanctuaries. Extensive excavations have been carried out and many buildings identified, although the visible remains date mostly from the second century. This was the city's most prosperous period when the frontier with barbarian Germany in this area had been advanced further to the east.

The town centre of Augst occupied most of the three *insulae*

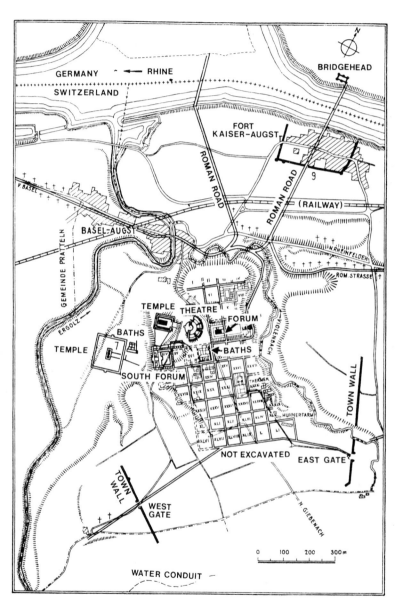

5   *Augst. Town Plan*

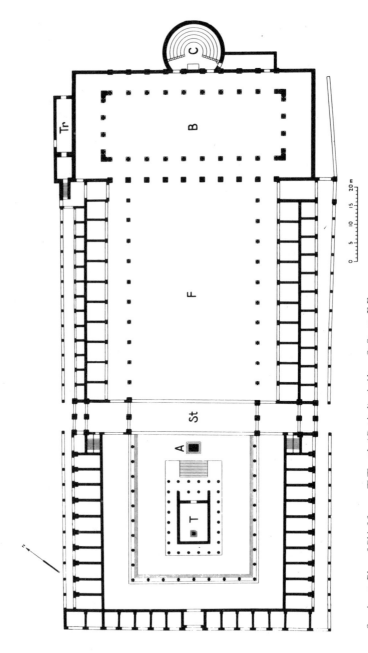

6 Augst. Plan of Chief forum. T Temple (Capitol). A Altar. St Street. F Forum. B Basilica of later period. C Curia of later period. Tr Steps

numbered XI–XIII, and was crossed by the main street. *Insula* XII in the centre was the forum with shops and colonnades on two sides(6). At one end was the basilica, B, a fine hall with interior galleries. At each end were the magistrates' courts. A semicircular room with tiered seats opening off the back is believed to be the council chamber of the *ordo* added in the third century.

At the other end of the forum the main street crossed the site, but was closed to wheeled traffic by a two-storeyed entrance on each side. The third *insula*, XI, was occupied by the fine temple, T, of the Capitoline triad, (see p. 190). Wide colonnades surrounded it on three sides. Colonnades and shops of varying size also opened onto the streets surrounding *insulae* XI–XIII on the outside. Behind the Capitoline temple is the theatre, probably built about A.D. 14, in the time of Augustus, and altered and extended twice, the last time being around A.D. 150. Contemporary with the later additions was another temple behind the theatre, also constructed on a high podium and surrounded by double porticos. The central part of the wall of the stage was removed, possibly so that the theatre audience could see religious processions approaching from the temple.

In many towns the forum was also the market place, but at Augst another market, the South Forum, in *insulae* XXI and XXII, was built on the steep slope near the theatre. This had shops on three sides and on the fourth, offices, probably of the market officials, behind a large hall. An entrance in the centre of the

7   *Augst. Reconstruction of Capitol*

8 *Augst. Reconstruction of part of the city. A Basilica, B Forum, C Capitol, D Theatre, E Temple, F South Forum, G site of Womens' Baths*

fourth side led out onto a terrace.

Near the South Forum, and possibly separated from it by an open space, are public baths (*insula* xvii) built about the middle of the first century A.D., and rebuilt on a larger scale with the plan shown here(*9*) in the second and third. Furnaces (marked P), burning wood or charcoal, heated hypocausts in rooms, I, T and C.

From the quantities of beads and hairpins found, it seems that these baths at Augst were used by the women especially as the dressing room, I, was heated and this is unusual. From I the bather made her way along a corridor to the unheated *frigidarium*, F, with a small swimming bath at v. Next came the warmed *tepidarium*, T, with a warm water basin at U and the *caldarium*, the hot room, at C. Water for its basins at R and S was

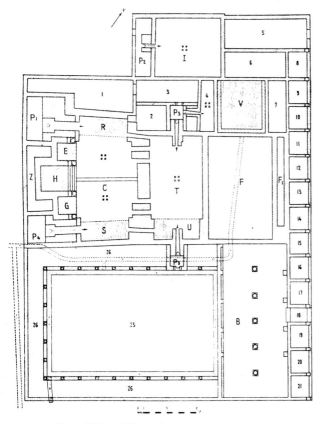

9   *Augst. Plan of Womens' Baths, late period*

heated in boilers placed over the furnaces at P_1 and P_4. The water in the smaller niches E and G and the plunge bath reached down steps at H, may have been cold, perhaps to revive the overheated, or slightly warmed by the heat of the room. Room 2 seems to have been the hottest of all where dry heat would produce profuse perspiration. The bather then made her way back, cooling off with a dip at V. Other rooms were used by the bath attendants.

In the earlier period a large open air swimming bath existed on the south side of the baths, but possibly the ladies rarely found the weather warm enough to use it so it was replaced by B, a large hall with a wooden floor and a row of five columns down the middle. This was probably a general meeting place reached through 6, 7 and the corridor F1, where friends could meet, gossip, and take refreshment, and even play games on wet days. On fine days these activities could go on in the large courtyard or garden surrounded by colonnades, 23. At 18 an exit led out to the street, which was lined by the small shops (8–17, 19–21). Baths for the men occupied *insula* XXXII and parts of XXVI and XXXVII.

In *insula* XXIII, south of the women's baths, there seems to have been an industrial area. In one room a cauldron was suspended over a tiled semi-circular hearth. Smoke from this was guided by

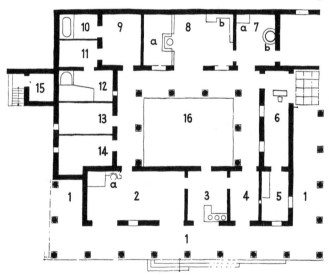

10 Augst. Plan of House. 1 Colonnade, 2 Workshop, 3 Tavern, 4 Entrance, 5 Entrance and reception room, 6 Office, 7 Kitchen, 8 Dining-room, 9–12 Baths, 13, 14 Bedrooms, 15 Furnace for heating baths, 16 Peristyle.

a flue at ground level into a small chamber where hams or sausages may have been smoked. Many animal bones were found here, and also a meathook and grindstones for the herbs used in the sausages. The Gauls are known to have enjoyed these products and to have exported them to Italy and elsewhere. In *insula* XXXIX a cellar containing 40 amphorae originally holding Spanish wine was found beneath one of a number of small dwellings. In a room above was a wall-painting showing two men carrying an amphora suspended from a pole.

On the corner of *insula* XXIII a small house has been excavated(*10*). Outside, passers-by were protected from the weather by the usual colonnade. An entrance, 4, leads into the peristyle, an open court with a portico on three sides and probably a garden in the centre. Opposite is the kitchen, 7, with the customary oblong hearth of masonry 60–90 cm (24–36 in.) high built up against the wall, with storage space for fuel underneath. On it the cook would place small iron grids and tripods supporting pots and metal vessels over heaps of glowing charcoal. Across the room is a round oven with domed top. This would be heated and then the ashes raked out and the bread or cakes put in(*11*).

The dining-room (*triclinium*), 8, is next to the kitchen. The three couches, on each of which reclined one or more diners, were grouped at *a*, round a small round table (*13*). On the other side of the room, *b*, shelves or tables acted as sideboards and silver or other household treasures were sometimes displayed here. The ladies when present did not recline but sat in chairs. In Gaul couches were not too popular and carved reliefs often depict husband and wife at dinner, both seated. The frontispiece shows them on a relief from Arlon just over the Belgian border, a chicken is being consumed and the table has three bandy legs and is covered with a cloth; glass vessels stand on another table in the background which is supported by a single leg decorated with an animal head; two maids are in attendance. In the nursery, however, life is less formal; the children gather round a cauldron and the boy on the right grabs the pet dog by his collar just in time; behind him another lad plays a tune on the double pipes.

Rooms 9–12 in the house at Augst are a small set of private baths heated by a furnace in 15; and 13 and 14 are bedrooms. The walls of the private rooms of the household were painted in various colours, the windows were glazed and the building was

11   Augst. Reconstruction of a kitchen

colour-washed on the outside. At 2, two large doorways opened
from the street into a workshop where metal-working or sausage-
making may have been carried on. No. 3 next door seems to have
been a tavern. The reconstruction, based on similar discoveries at
Pompeii, shows the counter with bowls of food inserted into it, a
row of jugs for measuring wine, a scale beam for weighing,
pottery cups, and hooks from which hang sausages(*12*).

In accordance with Roman law the cemeteries of Augusta
Raurica lay outside the city. A fine tombstone shows a man
wearing the Gaulish dress of tunic and hooded cloak, and holding
writing tablets. Below the inscription a pair of large scales is
depicted on which beams of timber are being weighed against
heavy stone weights, with more wood stacked up in the
background. This must be a portrait of a local timber-merchant.
A later stone, probably of the fourth century, records Eusstata,
sweetest wife of Amatus, who died aged 65; this lady was
probably a Christian.

48

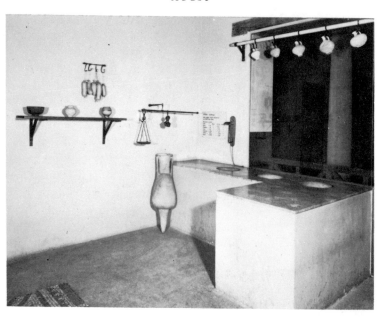

12 Augst.
Recon-
struction of
a tavern

13 Funeral
banquet,
Bonn

Augusta Raurica was almost completely destroyed in the invasions of the Alamanni in A.D. 259–60. As a result the surviving citizens began to build a wall round their city but for some reason this was never completed. The Rhine became the frontier and, about 300, a fort with massive walls and towers was built a short distance away. Later, when the city was in ruins, this fort was used as the residence of a Christian bishop.

The tombstone of L. Munatius Plancus, found at Gaeta in Italy, records that he founded two colonies. The second one, at Lyons (Lugdunum), was established on 9 October 43 B.C., a year after Augst, and replacing an *oppidum* of the Segusiavi. Owing to its position in central Gaul where two great rivers, the Rhône and the Saône meet, it soon became an important road junction. The colony was built on a high hill. On lower ground a Gaulish sanctuary already existed and more settlement developed here and on the opposite side of the Rhône. Downstream a flourishing business community established itself on the river bank and on an island. While much is known about the colony's gradual growth, research has been hampered by the fact that the whole area has been thickly populated ever since. The few surviving buildings include the theatre and the odeum (see p. 93). The reconstruction shows the situation in the second century with the colony in the centre upon the hill (*14*). The odeum and theatre with the temple of Cybele behind stand out in the middle. Outside the walls on the left is the circus. On the other side of the river, bottom right, is the amphitheatre.

Thirty km (19 miles) south of Lyons there was a colony at Vienne. One of the richest cities in Gaul it attracted wealthy inhabitants and there was some rivalry between it and Lyons. In fact the first Roman citizens of Lyons are said to have been people chased out of Vienne by the local tribe, the Allobroges.

Besides colonies, other towns flourished in southern France. Vaison, east of Orange, developed into a fine town built on the opposite side of the river Ouvreze, from an *oppidum* of the local tribe, the Vocontii. It remained one of their two tribal centres. Little is known of the earliest town which lies beneath the substantial remains of buildings dating from the late first century A.D. onwards. Baths and a theatre have already been uncovered; but the items of particular interest visible in Vaison are several

14   Lyons. Second century reconstruction. The city is on top of the hill. In the centre, the Odeum and Theatre with the Temple of Cybele behind. Outside the walls, top left, the Circus and aqueducts. Across the river Saône, bottom right, the Amphitheatre. Bottom left, the commercial and shipping areas on the island and the banks of the Rhône

houses, a pleasure garden and streets of shops. The House of the Messii in the street leading up to the theatre belonged to one of Vaison's leading families: painted walls, floors of pieces of marble or mosaic, and statuary including a fine marble head of Venus testify to the wealth of the inhabitants.

Near the house of the Messii is a large rectangular porticoed structure which seems to have been laid out as a public walk and garden. In the boundary wall square or semi-circular niches held statues including one of the Emperor Hadrian. The walls were painted with red panels framed in green above a black dado. In the centre of the garden was a lake and an island with a masonry foundation (possibly of a pergola, fountain, or small building)

51

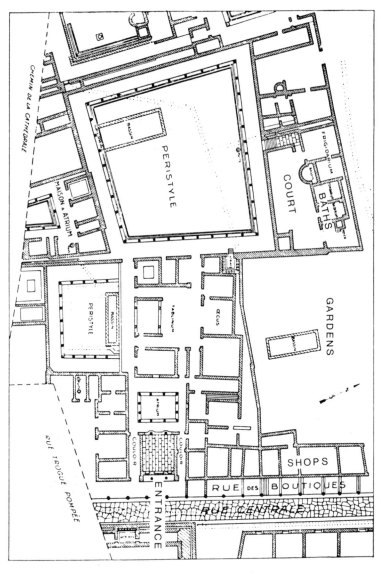

15   Plan of the House of the Silver Bust, Vaison

decorated with statuary and shrubs. A fragment inscribed 'Pompeia' has led to the site being known as the Portico of Pompey, possibly after Quintus Pompeius, one of Vaison's magistrates, who may have presented it to his fellow townsfolk. Continuing up the road to the theatre one of the structures found has been identified as a public lavatory with stone seats ranged over a channel of running water. Similar structures are known from many other towns including Pompeii and Timgad.

In another part of the town is the house of the Silver Bust (*15*). Its entrance is found in a street of shops and leads through a paved hall into an inner courtyard called the *atrium* which was open in the centre and surrounded by a roof supported by pillars. Two rooms lead to a small peristyle or courtyard, with colonnades on three sides and an oblong water tank or fish pond. Further west is another very large peristyle with room for an extensive garden and pool. Baths have also been found. Other rooms have not been certainly identified; they must include a dining-room and a kitchen. The silver bust from which the house takes its name was found among the ruins of the peristyle and may be a likeness of one of the inhabitants. An altar dedicated to Vulcan by Titus Julius Licinianus, and another with a relief of Vulcan with a hammer have been found, and also one dedicated to Fortuna by Veratianus. Small finds of bronzes, glass and pottery as well as traces of mosaics and wall-painting complete a

16 Street with shops, Vaison

picture of the town-house of a very Romanized Gaul. For its upkeep he may have depended on the rents of the small shops which line the street outside. These mostly consist of a single room but may have had a loft in the upper storey reached by a ladder. They were open fronted, and their sills still show the grooves for the folding wooden shutters which were pulled across and locked at night. Originally the street outside was bordered by the usual colonnaded walks, with steps at intervals to keep abreast with the gradient. Later the colonnade seems to have been incorporated into the shops which built out their side walls across it(*16*). Smaller houses in the same area include one with particularly interesting wall-paintings of hunters, lions, wild horses and a cheetah.

TOWNS IN GERMANY

No cities with the status of colony or *municipium* have been identified in northern France but several important tribal centres developed at Rheims, Amiens and Metz among others. Just over the present-day German frontier the sunny valley of the Moselle attracted inhabitants to Trier. Here several prehistoric religious sites and a number of hill-forts show pre-Roman occupation by the Germano-Celtic tribe of the Treveri. Subsequently a Roman auxiliary fort may have been constructed to control the river crossing. The fort attracted settlers and at the end of the first century B.C. a town began to develop, one of a number which started life as a result of direct encouragement from the Emperor Augustus. It was called Augusta Treverorum, Claudius granted it colonial status, and it became one of the major cities of the Roman Empire. Part of the walls with one great gate, the *Porta Nigra*, still survive(*17*), and also substantial remains of the bridge across the Moselle, baths and the amphitheatre. A great hall which belonged to the palace of the Emperor Constantine is incorporated in the walls of the 'Basilica', a church which now occupies the same site and gives a good idea of its size(*18*).

Further east in Germany we find evidence for the development of towns along the frontiers of the Rhine and the Danube. Two colonies are known in the province of *Germania Inferior* at Cologne and Xanten. Other towns also sprang up on the west bank of the Rhine, usually developing from the settlements of traders and shopkeepers outside the forts. Up river from Bingen, however, the pattern often changes, with Roman settlements succeeding

17   The Porta Nigra, Trier

native ones. The only military occupation consisted of forts
occupied during the campaigns of Drusus late in the first century
B.C., and fourth-century forts built when the Rhine was again the
frontier after the disasters suffered in the invasions of the previous
century.

Before this, many retired soldiers settled down to farming in
the fertile country across the river south of Wiesbaden, and as a
result small towns grew up where they could market their
produce. At Heddernheim (Nida) a cavalry fort was occupied
until the beginning of the second century when it was vacated
and its unit moved forward to the frontier at Eckzell. The
settlement outside the fort, however, continued to grow and
shows evidence of having been planned in *insulae*. A forum with
shops on two or three sides and probably a basilica at one end has
been identified, and an inscription found mentioning an *aedile*
and decurions of Nida. Other buildings included two sets of
baths, a theatre, and narrow rectangular houses, the earlier ones
timber-built and then replaced by masonry. Some houses may
have had two storeys, several had cellars. As the town grew it took
in the area occupied by the old fort. Outside, ribbon develop-

18   The Basilica, Trier

ment occurred along roads leading to bridges crossing the river Main. Much material from the fort was re-used in the building of the town walls at the beginning of the third century. The site was abandoned around A.D. 258 when the barbarian invasions made life there too precarious.

Another such town developed in Bavaria outside an early first-century fort at Kempten. The unit stationed there was moved forward to the Danube under Claudius, but the civil population remained and flourished. Its houses were stone-built from the first; a forum and basilica have been found and two sets of public baths. Conveniently adjoining the smaller baths was a large inn or *mansio* for officials and other travellers. A wide entrance led into the larger of two courtyards where carriages and wagons could be parked. Fifty rooms, including some on an upper storey with balconies, have been identified, and two annexes. The inn was built soon after A.D. 70 and was destroyed in 260. After this the town moved to the opposite bank of the river Iller.

AQUINCUM

Along the Danube the Romans set up camps in Pannonia which later became legionary fortresses at Carnuntum, (Deutsch Altenburg), 40 km (25 miles) west of Vienna, and at Aquincum (Budapest). Native settlements existed nearby. The fortresses attracted both natives and traders and soon settlements developed outside them. At first the natives were too poor to buy anything but peace brought them prosperity and fine towns grew up outside the military zones.

Aquincum was a port for river traffic and the frontier road, then studded with watch-towers, ran through both the civilian town and the fortress. Under Trajan, Pannonia was divided into two provinces with Carnuntum the capital of *Superior* and Aquincum, with Hadrian as its governor in A.D. 107, the capital of *Inferior*. In 124 Hadrian gave the town the status of a *municipium* and he may also have planned the governor's palace on an island in the Danube opposite the fortress. Carnuntum became a *municipium* at the same time.

Among the discoveries from the Aquincum *municipium* were fragments of surveying instruments, plane tables with plumb-lines and hinged stands, compasses, set squares and a primitive form of theodolite. They may have been used for the earliest town-planning when the scattered native daub houses and workshops were replaced by rather large *insulae*. The north and south gates were connected by a paved street with footpaths and colonnades, and on one side ran a water conduit fed by an aqueduct using water from the springs on the Buda slopes. Shops 15 m. (50 ft.) wide with store-rooms behind lined the street, one perhaps belonging to a lampseller who retailed the products of the lamp kilns found just outside the west gate. Another shop sold samian pottery imported from Gaul. The street crossing the town from east to west led out of the east gate down to the harbour. Where the two main streets crossed, the office of a money changer called Corinthus has been identified.

Other buildings included public baths and the meat market with shops on three sides and a small kiosk in the centre of its courtyard. Large store-rooms on either side of the wide gate may have held grain or pottery and some of the market scales and weights have been found. A water channel leading out from near the kiosk may show the whereabouts of the fish market. In the street near these markets was a third-century pottery workshop where cooking vessels and terracotta statuettes of such deities as Apollo, Venus, Attis and Abundantia were made. In the courtyard was a well from which part of the iron bucket chain was recovered, and a bronze lantern was found in the cellar. The pottery was sold in a shop across the road; living quarters including two heated rooms, and offices existed in a house next door. The limestone paving of the street outside was worn into ruts by the traffic.

In many cases these craftsmen's houses consisted of one or two shops opening onto the streets with living and working quarters behind. A laundry, a tannery, a glass blower's shop and several metal-working establishments have been identified. Most dwellings were developments of one-roomed rectangular buildings with a hearth. In some cases a central corridor leads in from a timber porch with rooms of various sizes opening off it. The walls consist of either a framework of timber resting on a stone foundation, the spaces filled in with clay, daub or stone, or masonry of stone with tile courses.

Other features of the civilian town were temples, a building believed to be a basilica and a large amphitheatre. Town walls were built at the beginning of the third century in response to attacks by the northern tribes after the city had been sacked several times between 167 and 180. Extensive rebuilding was necessary, and in 194 both Aquincum and Carnuntum were raised to the rank of colonies. A trade boom followed, largely in the hands of new settlers, mostly Greek traders. The soldiers spending their pay enabled city life to continue, but the troubled times led to a gradual decline. In 294 Aquincum was replaced as a provincial capital by Pecs (Sopianae) further away from the frontier. In the second half of the fourth century an attempt was made to strengthen the frontier with new small forts and other measures, but a shortage of manpower led to an increased use of mercenaries from the neighbouring tribes as garrisons. These barbarians tilled the lands near the forts; they were joined by their families, and they gradually absorbed what was left of the original city population.

Inscriptions record some of the magistrates of the civil town. An altar found in the sanctuary of the baths near the market appeals to Fortuna for her protection for the *municipium* and was dedicated in 193 by C. Valerius Valentinus, C. Julius Victorinus, and Publius Petronius Clemens. Three decurions, M. Ulpius Optatus, also a decurion of the *municipium*, dedicated an altar to Jupiter. Later inscriptions mention C. Julius Victorinus, a decurion, and M. Antonius Victorinus, *aedile*. In A.D. 259 another Julius Victorinus, *aedile*, and T. Flavius Lucianus, *quaestor*, had an altar dedicated to Diana Nemesis put up in her honour.

TOWNS IN THE EASTERN PROVINCES

In contrast to these Balkan provinces and the countries further west, for Greece, Asia Minor and Syria there is abundant literary evidence, both Greek and Jewish, and inscriptions in Latin, Greek, Aramaic, Nabataean and Palmyrene. The Greek language predominated although Claudius endeavoured to make a knowledge of Latin obligatory for Roman citizens, and Latin names are frequent. A few colonies of originally military character were found in unsettled areas, among them Beirut in the Lebanon, Ptolemais in Israel and later, under Hadrian, Aelia Capitolina on the site of Jerusalem, which had been destroyed in A.D. 70. The legions were normally stationed near cities, and it is only in central Jordan or on the Euphrates frontier that the familiar sequence of camp and settlement resulting in the development of town or colony occurs.

Elsewhere the royal lands of client kings became imperial estates when their kingdoms were absorbed. In the eastern provinces *municipia* are few and usually found in less civilized areas. Scholars believe that this is a proof that, owing to the respect that Romans had for Greek culture, the imperial government did not wish to force Romanization on its Greek-speaking subjects. Many cities were allowed to retain their ancient constitutions with councils and assemblies elected on a wider basis inherited from pre-Roman times. As a result the *ordo* was often larger than the ones noted in the west: in Syria it sometimes comprised 600 decurions and in Ephesus 450.

CORINTH

The Greek and Roman city of Corinth was built upon two natural terraces overlooking a fertile plain. Several miles away were the harbours at Lechaion on the Gulf of Corinth to the west for ships sailing the Adriatic Sea and at Kenchreai on the east for Aegean traffic. Cargoes could be portaged across from one side of the Isthmus to the other and traffic between Central and South Greece also had to cross it. The Greek city was destroyed by the Roman consul Mummius in 146 B.C. and lay desolate for a century. Julius Caesar refounded it as a colony in 44 B.C. Under Vespasian it was damaged by an earthquake but rebuilding followed and by the second century A.D. Corinth was the administrative capital of Greece, surpassing Athens in wealth and importance. Further destruction occurred from barbarian invasions in 267 and earthquakes in 375, and in 395 the city was burned by Alaric and the Goths.

The later history of Corinth tends to repeat this cycle of reconstruction following earthquakes or sackings, and as a result the Roman sites have been extensively robbed for building materials. Excavations, however, have revealed much, and many of the monuments mentioned by Pausanias on a visit to the city about A.D. 175 have been identified. To begin with the colonists used what was left of the older buildings but early in the first century A.D. Corinth began its transformation into a Roman city(*19*), with alterations in the Greek agora or market place. On the south side a row of shops with rooms behind and above had some partition walls removed to make larger rooms for the work of the new town administration. One horseshoe-shaped room (20) became the council chamber. At the east end of the row, is a small building (23) given by Cnaeus Babbius Philinus, a *duovir* of Corinth, which was altered fifty years later by his son or

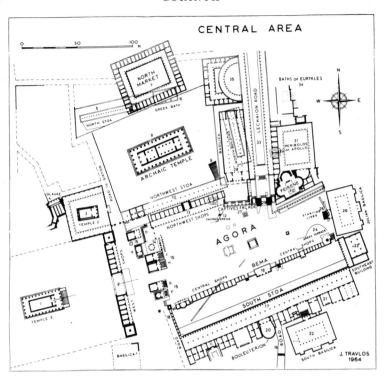

CENTRAL AREA

19 Plan of the central area. Corinth, 1 Roman temple, probably of the imperial cult, 4, 30 Fountains, 8 Greek temple of Apollo, 16 Bema or speaker's platform. 17 South Stoa or colonnade, 20 Bouleutherion (council chamber), 31 Colonnaded courtyard dedicated to Apollo

grandson. This may have housed the city archives.

In the centre of the agora was the dais (16) where the governor or other officials appeared to address the public; this was probably the place where St Paul came before the governor Gallio. It had a marble floor and rich decorations of carved marble. The west side was occupied by a series of temples. From Pausanias's description and excavation it seems that these included temples of Fortuna and a Pantheon dedicated to all the gods. In one may have stood a bronze statue of Apollo, and in front of another was a small circular building, its roof supported on eight Corinthian columns, also given by Babbius Philinus.

At the west end of the north side of the agora are shops replacing earlier Greek ones and behind them can be seen the

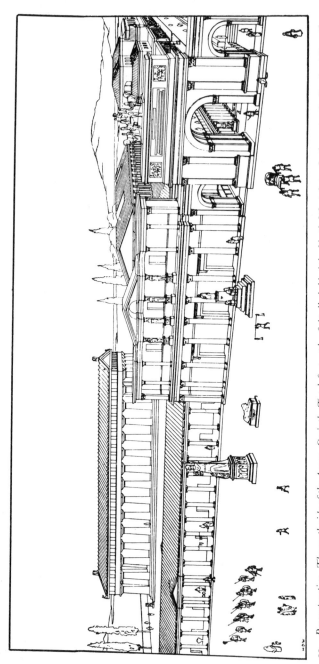

20 Reconstruction. The north side of the Agora, Corinth. Top left, temple of Apollo behind the North-West shops. In the centre the Captives' Facade with North Basilica behind. Further right, entrance leading to the Lechaion road

great temple of Apollo (8)(*20*), built in the sixth century B.C. and restored by the Romans. The reconstruction (*20*) shows it in the background behind the north-west shops in the agora. Next to the shops is an open court, its north wall decorated with a double row of marble columns; in the upper storey some columns were replaced by figures of barbarian captives standing on bases decorated with victory scenes. Behind this courtyard is the north basilica, and next to it the marble archway was the entrance to the agora, built in the first century. Pausanius relates that on top of it stood the gilded chariots of the sun god Helios and his son Phaethon. It led out on to the Lechaion road, paved, colonnaded and with more shops on the east side. Along the road on the left is the north basilica, one of the earliest Roman buildings in Corinth. Corinth is remarkably well off for basilican buildings, probably all used as law-courts or for other official purposes connected with the legal business of much of Greece.

Elsewhere in the city were the odeum, erected towards the end of the first century A.D. and rebuilt by Herodes Atticus; and the theatre, built on the site of the earlier Greek theatre, the wall between seats and orchestra decorated with paintings of gladiatorial scenes. Below a painted lion is a mis-spelled Greek account of the story of Androcles and the lion. An inscription records that an *aedile*, Erastus, paid for the floor of one of the stage buildings. The Greek tradition survives strongly in Roman Corinth especially in the orderly row of shops which are not associated with houses. In this they provide a contrast to the mixture of shops and houses noted in western cities, Vaison e.g.

TOWNS IN ASIA MINOR

Sailing across the Aegean Sea from the port of Kenchreai a Roman traveller would come to the province of Asia, one of the richest areas of the Empire. Much of it came under the control of Rome as a bequest from Attalus III, king of Pergamum, who died in 133 B.C. Under the Empire came two centuries of great prosperity disrupted by the usual third-century dislocations which were less severe here than in other areas. The territory included numerous ancient cities which continued their accustomed forms of local government under the general supervision, especially for finance and expenditure, of a governor residing at Ephesus. One such site was Pergamum itself where Attalus III and his predecessors had built a beautiful city on a series of terraces crowned by the Acropolis, an upper city at the top of a hill. Roman building activities were largely concerned with restoration although some fresh settlement developed to the west, and new theatres and a stadium were built. There were also new temples and the famous Asclepieum aroused much Roman interest (see p. 85).

Further south was Ephesus, a great port at the mouth of the river Cayster, which grew up as a Graeco-Oriental city devoted to the cult of the Anatolian goddess Cybele, called Artemis by the Greeks and, later, Diana by the Romans (see p. 202). With the exception of the Hellenistic walls and gates, the excavated areas here are mostly of Roman date. Temples, the library of Celsus, and the theatre are discussed elsewhere (see p. 81). Other buildings include a fine market or agora, four sets of baths, a fountain dedicated to Trajan complete with his colossal statue, and a large house built in the first century and spreading over five or more terraces, a storey on each. Here a first-century painting of Socrates and other treasures were discovered. Elsewhere two large blocks up to six storeys high have been found. The ground and first floors housed shops and offices, and the second floor cheap apartments; the higher floors contained sumptuous flats, and stairs led up to domestic quarters on the next floor. Elaborate fresh water and drainage systems communicated with drains under the passages. Ramps and steps led to the upper floors. Lavishly rich, full of beauty, and larger than all the other cities of Lydia and Ionia, Ephesus was also described as 'full of pipers, rascals and noise'.

TOWNS IN NORTH AFRICA
Lepcis Magna

In Tripolitania, several early Punic trading settlements of the fifth century B.C. or earlier developed into Roman cities. Lepcis Magna, with the advantages of a natural harbour and a well-watered caravan route to the interior, soon became a Roman road centre and flourished from the time of Augustus, probably becoming a *municipium* under Vespasian and a colony under Trajan. Architecturally it is possible to trace its development from the early Augustan buildings, some sited to fit in with Punic predecessors, to the fine new monumental quarter built under Septimius Severus and his successors. In the early Roman period native titles for magistrates and evidence of Punic religion

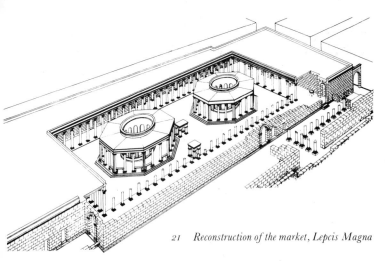

continue with the gradual Romanization of names. Bilingual inscriptions in Latin and Neo-Punic have been found, among them a dedication to Augustus in 8 B.C. by the *sufes* (*duovir*) Annobal Tapapius Rufus, son of Himilcho Tapapius, dating his gift of a market. The Tapapii were a wealthy family known from other inscriptions and Annobal Rufus also gave his city a theatre a few years later. Originally his market had colonnades but no shops; in the centre were two kiosks for the officials, and in A.D. 16 stalls were set up round them(*21*); busts of local dignitaries placed on shelves or in niches in the colonnades include one of Boncarth, son of Muthumbal, a first-century market official. Not very far from the theatre is a porticoed building called the chalcidicum erected in A.D. 11–12 as a gift of Iddibal Caphada Aemilius(*22*). Lepcis's first forum, laid out between 5 and 2 B.C., had new columns and fresh paving added in A.D. 54 by Caius, son of Hanno (G'y ben Hanno) in honour of his grandson. Both inscriptions are repeated in Neo-Punic.

Volubilis

Extensive remains survive from a number of other Roman cities in North Africa among them Cyrene and Sabratha in Libya, Carthage and Dougga in Tunisia, and Tebessa, Timgad and Djemila in Algeria.

In Morocco a Roman town with an unusual history is still being excavated at Volubilis. The pre-Roman inhabitants seem to have been influenced by Punic civilization and Neo-Punic inscriptions have been found on the site. In 25 B.C. northern

22 *Iddibal Caphada Aemilius, Lepcis Magna*

Morocco and western Algeria formed the Roman client kingdom of Mauretania ruled by Juba II and his wife Cleopatra Selene, daughter of Cleopatra and Mark Antony. Both had been educated in Rome and together they built Cherchel (Iol Caesarea) and Volubilis. Juba was a connoisseur of the arts and many fine bronze and stone statues found on those two sites may have belonged to him. He was a loyal supporter of Rome and fought hard during his long reign to repel attacks by the nomadic mountain tribes who raided his kingdom.

In A.D. 40 the Emperor Gaius (Caligula) murdered Juba's son Ptolemy, and after some rebellion the kingdom was added to the Empire. The people of Volubilis, however, supported Rome in quelling the resistance. Their army was led by Marcus Valerius Severus, son of Bostar and husband of Birra, daughter of Izelta. Bostar appears to be a Punic name, the other two are probably Libyan. An inscription put up in his honour in both Punic and Latin by the *ordo* but paid for by his wife, describes him as a magistrate with the Punic title of *sufes*. He was also the first priest of the imperial cult in Volubilis. After the rebellion he led a deputation to the new emperor, Claudius, seeking help for

66

repairs to war damage. His embassy was brilliantly successful: not only was Volubilis relieved of taxation for the next ten years but the community was given Roman citizenship, probably with the status of *municipium*, which marked the degree of Romanization it had already attained. Another inscription relates that the inhabitants put up a statue to Claudius as a thank offering.

Volubilis seems to have prospered and by the mid-second century fine houses and public buildings arose there. Pre-existing structures prevented the development of the regularity of the usual Roman town plan, and when the walls were built in response to the threat of raids from the interior during the reign of Marcus Aurelius, room seems to have been left for refugees and their animals in emergencies. Outside, houses with gardens were built on the banks of the local streams or wadis. The town reached its highest peak early in the third century when the procurator M. Aurellius Sebastenus laid the foundation stone of a triumphal arch in honour of the Emperor Caracalla. This was an expression of the city's gratitude for various favours bestowed on the African provinces by Caracalla and his father Septimius Severus. Little is known of the public buildings before the time of the Severi. The forum with a basilica occupying one side lies above earlier structures, and the capitol dated by an inscription to 217 would also have had a predecessor. Other temples and several sets of baths have been excavated and a mountain spring 1 km ($\frac{1}{2}$ mile) away seems to have provided an abundant water supply for an aqueduct, backed up by rain-water cisterns.

The notable feature of Volubilis, however, is the discovery of a number of luxurious houses. One very large establishment which includes many small rooms as well as some palatial ones may be the governor's palace with the small rooms used as offices. Earlier buildings which lie beneath it may be the remains of the palace of Juba II. The house of Orpheus, unlike most of the large houses, lies in the southern half of the town in the area of pre-Roman occupation. Excavations have revealed expansion taking place during three main periods in which, perhaps, a Romanized family of oil merchants added to their home and rebuilt it with as Roman a plan as possible, much inconvenienced by the existence of earlier walls. There are several entrances, the chief one leading into an *atrium* with a rectangular water tank; this had an amphora buried at each corner as a refuge for the gold fish when the tank was cleaned. In the room adjoining is the mosaic from which the house takes its name, unfortunately much damaged; it depicts Orpheus richly dressed and surrounded by animals including a stag, an elephant, and a tiger, and birds such as the owl and peacock. On the east side are the family's private rooms, some with hypocausts, and a summer dining-room opening on to a colonnade with four fountains and mosaics of birds and dolphins. Another dining-room had gaily painted walls and a mosaic of nine dolphins. Nearby was the kitchen with a masonry oven, a water tank, and a niche for the household gods. This house had its own private bath suite. Used water was channelled to flush the latrines into sewers beside the street. Provision was made for oil manufacture with first one press and later two, and also tanks and store rooms.

The north-eastern area of the town is still being excavated. It seems to have been primarily a well-to-do residential area, with houses lying behind the rows of shops, many with colonnades in front, which lined the streets. The entrance to each house was often in the centre of a block of shops through a large doorway leading first into a paved vestibule and then into the peristyle. Sometimes, however, the entrance was at one end with a narrower opening into one corner of the peristyle, possibly this was an extra precaution to prevent thieves gaining admission to the heart of the house. The doorways show evidence of elaborate bolts and bars suggesting that security was an important consideration.

The chief reception room was either on the opposite side of the peristyle to the vestibule, or at one side. On another side was the dining-room planned so as to catch the winter sunshine. Some houses have an *atriolum*, a small court with a tank in the centre leading off the peristyle and surrounded by smaller rooms which were probably the family's private quarters. The 25 or so houses excavated in this area show that their plan is different from that of a typical Roman house as, apart from one or two exceptions, there is no *atrium*. The *atrium* is largely replaced by the peristyle which seems to have been the centre of activity rather than a peaceful retreat, although elaborate water tanks and fountains in the open space at the centre helped to keep it cool and pleasant. The *atriolum* had to be developed to give the family privacy and seclusion. Scholars working at Volubilis see in these arrangements a fusion between elements from both Greek and Roman house-planning.

From the site of the later Triumphal Arch of Caracalla, the main street of Volubilis continues to the east gate. On its north side are six of the recently-excavated houses. No. 1, the house of the Labours of Hercules, was the first to be built, dating from the late second century. It is named after the subject of a mosaic floor and has a number of fine rooms with other mosaics, and a large suite of baths; it is possible that the owner let some of this accommodation for dinner parties. No. 5 in the row was the next to be built early in the third century, and then nos. 2 and 3. Soon after no. 4 was fitted into the empty space between nos. 3 and 5; on the street front there was only room for a long narrow vestibule with a single entrance, and two shops, one perhaps selling fishing tackle, the other possibly pottery; much of the house was occupied by oil works. At the end of the reign of Caracalla shops appeared on the south side of the street which runs behind these houses, and during the third century the houses expanded to the north until they gradually absorbed the shops.

Further east, on the other side of the street, comes the House of the Gold Coins which comprises more than 45 rooms. Built about the beginning of the third century it may originally have been smaller but soon grew in a westerly direction to include a whole *insula*, possibly incorporating earlier buildings. Its owner seems to have been a rich man with fastidious tastes whose commercial interests included the rents of the shops which occupy the street fronts on two sides of his house. At one corner three rooms and a passage, probably with an upper storey, may have been let as a separate apartment. The western part of the house was used for a large oilworks with, next door, two corn-mills, an oven and a kneading trough proving the existence of a bakery. Beside this and behind it are paved areas belonging to stables with space for carts to unload; drinking troughs were discovered there and three semi-circular mangers were found fixed to the wall.

In contrast to the successful businessman of the House of the Gold Coins, several sites seem to have been occupied by people with no commercial interests. One example is the House of the Cortège of Venus tucked away from traffic in a side street. In a room next to the vestibule were found four altars for the worship of the household gods. The peristyle is unusually large with a small garden which has a central water tank running across it widening at each end to give an I-shaped plan. The porticos surrounding this have mosaic floors mostly with geometric designs, but one shows a chariot race between ducks and peacocks. The mosaicists, obviously copying from a pattern book, have not fitted their design into the available space very successfully. The famous mosaic shows Venus and the three Graces on board a ship with Cupids climbing the rigging and Tritons swimming around with baskets of flowers. Remains of furniture, including couches, were found here decorated with a bronze mule's head and a bust of Silenus. Other fine bronzes may be survivors from King Juba's collection. Pieces of a bronze water-heater were also found. This house may date from the second half of the second century. Later, baths were added and the colonnaded pavements beside the street outside were incorporated into the house.

A feature of especial interest at Volubilis is the clear picture revealed of the distribution of water supplies from the aqueducts through a network of lead pipes in underground conduits with pipes leading into the peristyle watertank in each house. A similar system of drainage channels carried away sewage. House alterations led to complications, and in the third century new outlets had to be constructed for the drains from some of the houses in the main street. Several public lavatories have also been identified.

Not much is known of the trades carried on in the 119 shops of north-east Volubilis. Those along the main street may have sold jewellery, textiles and other luxuries. Seven bakeries have been found, often placed at the corner of an insula. Apparently the majority of the shopkeepers did not live in or above their shops. At night they put up their sliding shutters or locked their doors and went home to one of the small dwellings found elsewhere in the town.

Volubilis's peaceful and prosperous existence as a Roman city, untroubled by earthquakes, fires or serious warfare seems to have ended about A.D. 284–5 when the Romans were no longer able to hold the frontier against the tribes of the hinterland. After Diocletian's reorganization it lay outside the boundaries of the Empire. Several inscriptions, however, suggest that traces of local government by magistrates lingered on in the city even into the sixth century.

4

Home life, education and recreation

While much can be learnt of the domestic habits of the Romans at home in Italy, and the ceremonies connected with birth, growing up and marriage, far less information is obtainable about these subjects from the provinces, and it is not easy to recreate the daily life of their inhabitants. We know most about work in shops, in the mines or on the land, and these topics will be considered in the next two chapters. The life of the family out of working hours, however, can only be dimly glimpsed.

THE DAILY ROUND

The Gaulish author Ausonius in the late fourth century composed a poem he called 'The Daily Round' (*Ephemeris*) of which only his account of the morning survives. At the time he wrote he was probably an elderly man living on his Bordeaux estate after a distinguished career as a professor of rhetoric and a landowner. He had held important government posts and was for ten years tutor to Gratian, son of the Emperor Valentinian I. He had become a Christian but he was also deeply steeped in the old pagan religion and learning.

In the course of the poem he wakes and describes his dreams. Some are peaceful visions of the law courts, a banquet or a theatrical performance; others are nightmares of war, imprisonment or the horrors of the amphitheatre. The poem begins as he reproaches his young servant for oversleeping, and bids him bring water for washing, and his clothes. Then the chapel must be opened and a long prayer offered. Next the boy must bring his cloak and he will visit friends. However he then realizes it is already 10 o'clock so he sends the servant to invite five friends to lunch instead (six was considered to be the ideal number for an informal meal). Ausonius meanwhile visits his cook and tells him to taste and season carefully the dishes already bubbling away in bronze or pottery pans on iron gridirons over glowing charcoal. The kitchen, no doubt, was full of hurrying servants preparing the meal. Finally he summons his secretary, who is so expert that he can almost write down Ausonius's thoughts before he utters them. From other sources we may guess that the afternoon was spent in talking or out of doors, followed by a visit to the baths.

Early in the evening dinner would be served. The Roman interest in food was probably shared by those provincials who could afford it. A poor man's diet might be largely cereals made into a kind of porridge, or bread, with a few vegetables, cheese or fish. Ausonius indeed remarks elsewhere that mussels make a delightful luncheon dish. His dinner, however, would probably have a three-course menu beginning with hors-d'oeuvres, mostly vegetables, eggs, snails or shellfish. Next would come the main course with a choice from a succession of dishes including fish such as turbot, poultry, game or meat. Venison or wild boar were among the party favourites. A cookery book published in the late fourth or fifth century included recipes probably invented some time earlier by Apicius, a famous gourmet. Among them are 17 different ways of cooking sucking pig, and directions for more exotic dishes including ostrich and peacock. A simpler recipe was ham boiled with dried figs and three bay leaves: when almost cooked, the skin was removed and incisions made which were filled with honey; then the ham was covered with a paste of flour and oil, put in the oven and baked. (Quantities suggested for modern cooks are 3 lbs. of ham or gammon and $\frac{1}{2}$ lb. of figs, with 1 lb. of flour for the pastry. Baking time is well over an hour in a medium oven, pre-heated.) Fruit and perhaps honey cakes might conclude the meal. With it was served wine cooled with snow or mulled with spices.

Ausonius also gives us a glimpse of family life in a series of poems describing 30 of his deceased relations, including his children's parents-in-law. The impression he conveys is of a serene and unostentatious existence: the women were careful housewives, the men were friendly and often active in public affairs. All were devoted to learning. Pride of family was one of their strongest emotions; distinguished ancestors were long remembered. Ausonius's father, for whom he had a great respect, was a physician at Bordeaux. He seems to have had less affection for his mother. Apparently he was brought up by a strict grandmother and cherished by several aunts. His maternal grandfather was a tribal aristocrat who came from near Lyons. An expert astrologer, Ausonius's horoscope, correctly predicting his rise to a consulship, was found among the old man's papers after his death. At the age of 24 Ausonius married Sabina. Their first child died when a baby; after the birth of a son and a daughter Sabina died aged 27. In the poem written in her memory 36 years later, Ausonius still mourns for her. Calling her his grief and his glory, he remains lonely; he never married again.

MARRIAGE

As was the case with most Roman marriages, Ausonius's bride would have been chosen by his parents, his father in particular, although with a daughter the mother would expect to be consulted. The advice of influential friends was often sought in arranging a suitable match. For example, about A.D. 155 the writer Apuleius, while on a journey to Egypt, was taken ill at Oea (Tripoli) and visited by a friend. The friend confided to him his anxiety about his widowed mother who was being encouraged to make an unsuitable marriage, and took Apuleius to meet her. Finding her to be an attractive and wealthy lady, Apuleius married her himself. Other members of the family resented this and accused Apuleius of having won her by magic. A trial followed in which he was triumphantly acquitted.

Once the betrothal was arranged, gifts were exchanged, the bride's dowry discussed, an agreement to marry was signed, and a kiss followed. Rings and pendants decorated with two clasped hands are sometimes found and these were probably bought for such occasions. For the wedding, in Rome the bride had her hair elaborately dressed, she wore a white wool tunic with a girdle tied with an elaborate knot, and a wreath of marjoram on her head. The short oblong wedding-veil was orange coloured and did not cover the face. Orange shoes were also worn. The wedding itself was a civil ceremony with the bridegroom coming to the bride's house in procession. The bridesmaid led forth the bride and joined their hands together. The marriage contract was signed, many of the guests acting as witnesses, everyone wished the couple well and a feast followed. In the evening the pair were escorted to their new home, and the bride rubbed oil and fat on the doorposts and wound wool round them; she was then carried over the threshold.

Weddings are occasions when old traditions die hard and other native customs must also have played a part in the provinces. We can only speculate about the details of clothing, food, charms to ensure good luck and avert the evil eye, and offerings to local deities which were carefully prepared for such weddings as that of the shipowner, Blussus, at Mainz and his wife Menimane (74).

CHILDREN

Children were cherished, there seems little doubt of that. They appear frequently on reliefs and tombstones, some of them very crude memorials but the best a parent could afford. A small relief from Vertault shows three Gallic mother-goddesses illustrating current views on child care(23). The lady on the left supports a swaddled infant on her knee; the central figure may have either a clean swaddling cloth or a towel spread out on her lap and the one on the right holds a bowl and a sponge. On the side of a third-century tombstone dedicated to Amma Severina at Cologne is a swaddled baby in a cradle or carry-cot; another relief at Beaune shows an infant under a coverlet with the pet dog asleep at the foot. The framework of a wooden cradle on rockers survives at Herculaneum.

23   Tombstone of Laetus's daughter. Bordeaux

24   Mother Goddesses. Vertault

Infant mortality was high. In Aquincum there is the tombstone of Veturia, wife of a centurion, who died aged 27; of her six children only one survived. At Bordeaux a father and mother mourned for the 16-month-old Tiberius, as does another father, Laetus, for the small girl depicted with a pet cock which has just grabbed the tail of the kitten struggling in her arms(24). At Bourges Priscinus is shown on his tombstone in his father's arms.

On another Bordeaux tombstone Aveta appears, mirror in hand, accompanied by her daughter and lamented by her mother Cintugena(25). A Lyons grandmother was more fortunate: when she died aged 84 she had five grandchildren and her lively affection for them made life sweet for her during 18 years of widowhood. Grown-up children are also recorded at Lyons where two girls lament a dead sister dearer to them than life, and a mother mourns two sons, one dead on a distant voyage. Less common are memorials to a very respectful son-in-law or an excellent mother-in-law.

Unwanted children, girls in particular, might be abandoned at birth and their pathetic little skeletons are occasionally found, especially in slave quarters and in the settlements of poorer folk. Such foundlings were sometimes rescued, and the emperors and other rich men gave money for their care. Inscriptions mention foster children and a number recording their gratitude to their patrons are known from North Africa. At Timgad, Asiaticus, a foundling, commemorated his well-deserving patron Hypnus Pius. On the other hand Ulpius Optatus had to put up the tombstone for M. Ulpius Superatus, his sweetest foster-child, aged 9.

25   Tombstone of Aveta. Bordeaux

HOUSEHOLD PETS, TOYS AND GAMES

Both children and adults are portrayed accompanied by pets, usually dogs or birds. Cats and hares appear less frequently, but at

Bordeaux the six-year-old Aurelia Satyra haṣ her cat on her lap; and a boy with a whip in one hand at Dijon watches his cat walk up his other arm. At Bourges, Graccha, aged 16 months, appears as a slightly older child holding a basket containing three puppies with their mother sitting at her feet, and reliefs of small boys also depict their dogs. In Germany, Volcius Mercator, commemorated by his wife and daughter, is shown with his small dog waiting patiently behind him, and Blussus's wife has her dog on her knee (74).

Toy animals were as loved by children then as now and survive made of bronze and pottery. Babies' rattles, rag dolls or jointed wooden dolls, the best with Antonine hairstyles, miniature pots and pans and the dolls' house furniture for little girls, and hoops, whips and tops for the boys have all been found. Small carriages drawn by goats, and model versions drawn by birds, horses, or other animals on wheels and pulled along by a string were also favourites. Swings and see-saws were provided and familiar games such as blind man's buff, hide and seek, or leap frog, all seem to have been played in the Roman Empire. People of all ages took part in ball games at home in the courtyard or in the *palaestra* at the baths. Marbles and dice are quite often found.

SCHOOLING

Among the wealthier classes the education of the child was a matter for earnest consideration. From the first century onwards the private tutor tended to be replaced by schools with pupils usually gathered round a teacher in a room off the forum. As a result, market days may have had to be holidays as the noise would have drowned the teacher's voice. A Narbonne relief may show such a schoolroom lit by two windows with two seated schoolmasters and a dozen children ranged on benches; two latecomers just arriving seem to be trying to hide behind a master's chair. From the age of six or seven, boys and girls went to school daily attended by their pedagogues, slaves who had also had some teaching so that they could superintend their charges' activities and hear their lessons. Libanius, in the fourth century, describes a schoolboy's day in Antioch ending in a visit to the baths and supper. In Gaul at this time Ausonius was encouraging his grandson not to fear school discipline. These authorities are comparatively late, but the pattern of Roman education, once established, changed little.

Up to the age of eleven most of a child's lesson time was devoted to reading and writing. The alphabet was learnt letter by letter then written on wooden tablets, either by pricking out the letters on a wax surface or using a split reed pen and ink. Evidence of writing practice on scraps of used papyrus or of scratching with a stylus on any bit of broken pot, slate or tile which came to hand is also found. Good second-century examples of the Greek alphabet which may be teachers' copies are known from Egypt from Thebes, and the Latin alphabet scratched on a tile has been found at Carnuntum. The Pannonian villa of Eisenstadt produced another tile with the alphabet of single letters also used with the vowels, Ba, Ca, Be, Ce, etc. Eventually the pupil began to read short sentences and selected passages were learnt by heart or written down as dictation. Discipline was harsh although Quintilian, writing on education in the first century in terms with which we would agree today, was already disapproving of corporal punishment and setting high personal standards for teachers. From Trier the well-known relief of a school scene shows the master grimly regarding a latecomer; and at Arlon a teacher, stick in hand, gazes out uncompromisingly (*26*).

These primary school masters usually possessed only mediocre educational attainments. Their pupils learned to read, write and count, and for many children education ended at this level. Otherwise, at twelve the child was promoted to the school of the *grammaticus*, a man of wider learning. There the pupil studied literature in greater detail. Ausonius sums it up as 'Read thoroughly whatever is worth remembering'. Clear speech and

26   Schoolmaster. Arlon

correct pronunciation were insisted on. Frequent pauses were made to discuss grammar or explain the meanings of words. Allusions to poetry, mythology, history, geography or philology were carefully noted, so that a store of general knowledge was acquired.

Tombstones of *grammatici* are not infrequent. Domitius Isquilinus from Cordoba taught Greek literature and lived to be 101. While some well-known masters might attract numerous pupils, the *grammatici* were often poorly paid. Ausonius contrasts the Greek *grammatici* of Bordeaux, patient, earnest teachers making a small profit, with Marcellus at Narbonne whose crowded classes brought him wealth, 'a *grammaticus* of very scant deserving'. Imperial encouragement of teachers led to their exemption from taxation, and in some cases, as at Tritium (Spain), salaries were paid by municipalities.

At sixteen the promising scholar went on to study rhetoric with a *rhetor*. Public speaking was an important part of Roman life for the decurion or anyone holding office, so skill in declamation and the ability to write a persuasive speech were essential for an educated man. Outside Italy most is known of the *rhetores* of Gaul, a country where oratory had long been highly regarded and where Ogmios, the god of poetry and eloquence, was described as an old man drawing men to him by fine gold chains leading from his tongue to their ears. Inscriptions referring to *rhetores* from other provinces include one from Cadiz.

In newly-conquered areas education was used as part of the deliberate policy of Romanization. The sons of the local aristocracy were gathered together by the general Sertorius in Spain in 79 B.C., and gradually a network of schools spread over the Iberian peninsula. In Africa, Latin was introduced in Caesar's time and schools developed, and the same was true of Gaul. Suetonius in his life of Caligula mentions a military school for young German hostages near the Rhine, and Tacitus records Agricola setting up schools in Britain.

Many pupils learnt Greek as well as Latin. In Gaul the Greek colonies at Marseilles and other places produced eminent teachers. There is evidence for Greek spoken by Celts on the Atlantic coast, and in the second century the churches at Lyons and Vienne commissioned lives of the martyrs written in Greek. Only in the fourth century did the interest in Greek die out. Greek settlement in Sicily and Cyrenaica also produced an early interest in Greek in Africa. Apuleius at Oea in the mid-second century could poke fun at scholars ignorant of Greek. Vetidius Juvenalis at Thubursicu Numidarum a little later on sent his two sons, both learned in Latin and Greek, to Carthage to complete their education. Alas, both died. Interest in Greek waned however, and by the end of the third century a Thubursicu tombstone commemorates Nonius Marcellus, a *grammaticus* teaching only Latin.

Besides Latin and Greek, native languages survived in most provinces so that some individuals must have been bilingual or even trilingual. These languages were not always written down so it is difficult to estimate their importance. Probably they were mostly found in country districts while townsfolk and traders soon acquired enough Latin for practical purposes. As the Druids of pre-Roman Gaul disapproved of writing and transmitted their learning orally to the young, their power was largely broken when the Roman schools opened. Some Gaulish inscriptions using the Latin alphabet survive, mostly religious but including lists on potsherds made in the samian potteries (see p. 177). Similarly in Phrygia Greek characters were used for third-century Phrygian inscriptions, often accompanied by a Greek translation. In North Africa some early inscriptions written in a Libyan alphabet of 23 characters survive, while others are in neo-Punic script, sometimes with Latin translations.

CENTRES OF LEARNING

Famous teachers attracting students from far afield settled in some cities, and these were the ancestors of later universities. Besides Rome, Athens and Alexandria, Carthage, where Apuleius and Vetidius Juvenalis's sons studied, was one such centre. In Gaul Autun was famous for its schools from the time of Tiberius. Destroyed by roving bands of outlaws at the end of the third century, Constantius Chlorus restored it after urgent pleadings from its teachers and citizens. Lyons, where literary competitions date back to Caligula, was another important centre. Others included Vienne, Rheims, Besançon, etc. In the fourth century Ausonius lists professors at Bordeaux with several hundred students. Soon after Autun was supplanted by Trier. In the East, Antioch and Ephesus were among famous centres of learning. The study of law and the training of the lawyer and advocate were the special Roman contributions to education. Important law schools grew up at other places besides Rome,

notably at Beirut which developed a five-year course. Carica-
tures of teachers and readers are not infrequent. A number were
found in a child's grave at Colchester and another one comes
from Vechten in Holland.

The Latin literature studied in the Roman schools of this
period included Virgil, Horace, Ovid, Terence, Cicero and
Seneca, with Homer and Menander still pre-eminent among the
Greeks. Virgil was particularly admired and quotations, such as
the first two lines of the *Aeneid* probably scratched by a schoolboy
on a tile from Italica (Spain), are sometimes found. The choice of
subjects for mosaic pavements also reflects literary interests e.g.
the heads of Homer, Virgil and the Muses on the floor designed
by Monnus at Trier, the famous mosaic depicting Virgil with two
Muses and Book I of the *Aeneid* open on his knee from Sousse, or
the scenes with Dido and Aeneas on the mosaic from the Low
Ham villa.

BOOKS AND LIBRARIES

Books were treasured possessions and educated men gradually
built up their own libraries. Skilled copyists, usually slaves, were
at work in Rome and probably in other cities, some publishers
employing perhaps 50 at a time. New speeches or poems by
authors such as Cicero or Martial were speedily copied and
distributed. Prices were reasonable. School texts seem to have
been readily obtainable. The existence of trade in secondhand
books is shown by Libanius's account of attempts to burgle his
library, one treasured copy of Thucydides being retrieved from a
stall in the market at Antioch. To lend a book to another reader
was a sure proof of friendship.

Public libraries were either the gifts of emperors or wealthy
townsfolk or built at municipal expense. By the fourth century
Rome had 29. Seven are known from other Italian cities, six from
Greece, and several from Asia Minor, North Africa, and Egypt.
Famous libraries at Alexandria and Pergamum date back to
Hellenistic times. Titus Flavius Pantainos and his son and
daughter built a library at Athens soon after A.D. 100. Its
decorations probably included a sculpture of Homer between
personifications of the *Iliad* and *Odyssey*. Greek inscriptions
include part of the library regulations: 'No book shall be
removed since we have taken an oath to that effect. Open from
the first hour to the sixth, i.e. from early morning until noon.

Book borrowing, forbidden here, was permissible in some libraries. Later in the second century Hadrian founded a larger library in Athens, leading off a courtyard with a garden and a pool.

The best-preserved library buildings still surviving are at Ephesus and Timgad. The first commemorates a distinguished Ephesian, Caius Julius Celsus Polemaeanus, and was begun by his son Aquila about A.D. 110 and finished by his heirs about 135.

27 *Library of Celsus. Ephesus*

81

The lofty hall was entered up steps and through a portico. Inside the walls were lined with book cupboards. Two tiers of galleries with more cupboards were reached by stairs in the thickness of the walls. Other stairs led down to the mausoleum where Celsus lay buried in a lead casket in a white marble sarcophagus. His statue no doubt stood in the vaulted apse in the library above. Aquila left 25,000 denarii for the purchase of books and the upkeep of the library. Nearby was probably the auditorium where rhetors and poets gave lectures and readings.

The main library at Timgad was a semicircular hall placed at one end of the usual courtyard with porticos. It had a central niche in which probably stood a statue of Minerva. The entrance could be closed with a large grille, probably preferred to a door to ensure that the library was well-ventilated and the books preserved from damp. Bronze medallions with busts of authors may have decorated the walls above the book cupboards. Benches and tables were probably provided for readers, and small rooms leading off the courtyard may have been stack rooms. Quintianus Flavius Rogatianus left 400,000 sesterces to pay for the erection of this building.

MEDICINE

Rome's ideas of doctors and medical schools originally came from the Greeks. The first systematic instruction was probably given at Alexandria and centres then grew up in Rome, Laodicea, Smyrna, Pergamum, Corinth, Marseilles, Lyons and Bordeaux. Physicians took pupils as apprentices under a form of contract and the army also needed doctors. From these sources the Roman state medical service developed with so many doctors employed by each city. Like teachers they were exempt from taxes. They could accept fees but were expected to treat the poor free of charge. Inscriptions mentioning doctors are known from Spain and France. Women doctors are also sometimes mentioned as at Nîmes and Lyons. At Merida, Julia Saturnina aged 45 is mourned by her husband Cassius Philippus as an incomparable wife, the best of doctors and a holy woman. Gynaecology was probably her speciality.

Medical students studied the Hippocratic corpus, a collection of writings some centuries old, on surgery, dietetics, epidemics, natural science and philsophy collected by the Alexandrian school. Celsus, a first-century Roman, compiled his *De Medicina* on similar subjects, mixing good practical advice with some strange theories. The elder Pliny and Dioscorides listed drugs and herbs useful in illness. In the second century Galen, after useful experience as physician to gladiators in Asia Minor, studied in Greece and Alexandria, and then practised in Rome and Pergamum. He added new knowledge about anatomy and physiology and his works were still studied throughout the Middle Ages. Every household, no doubt, also had its own stock of simple remedies. Medical treatment included rest, diet, blood-letting, emetics and purging.

Experience after battles or gladiatorial combats taught the doctors much about surgery, and operations on fractures, ampu-tations, tonsils, goitres and hernias are known to have been carried out. Surgical instruments made of bronze or the best iron, preferably from Noricum, sometimes survive. A cremation burial of the first half of the second century found at Bingen is probably that of a surgeon because with it were three cups for bleeding hung on a stand, scalpels, often several combined with a spatula for spreading ointment, tweezers, a round saw-toothed tool for drilling bone, hooks, probes and surgical needles. A model bronze hippopotamus has a snake, the symbol of healing, on his back(28). Medicines were carried in bronze boxes with sliding lids, divided into compartments each with its own lid. One from Mainz has a snake twined round a laurel tree on its lid inlaid in silver.

Conjunctivitis, opthalmia, glaucoma, cataract and other eye troubles were well-known to the Romans and treated with fomentations, drops and ointment. Eye-salves were made up as solid sticks of ointment stamped with the oculist's name. Many of these stamps, sometimes also mentioning the eye-trouble, have been found in the western provinces, particularly in north-east France, and in the valleys of the Loire and Rhine. Eleven from Bavai and ten from Rheims suggest a lively trade in remedies in the markets, especially as some names recur in different places.

At Rheims the oculist G. Firminius Severus died towards the end of the second century and his equipment in a wooden chest was buried with him. It includes his stamp, forceps, and hooks for turning back eyelids, spatulas and olive-ended probes for spreading salve, scalpels, needles, a small drill, scales, ointment jars, and remains of ointments. These were analysed and were found to show traces of mineral substances such as mercury and zinc oxide still in use today, mixed in honey, gum, myrrh or fat of some kind. The practice seems to have been a lucrative one as several of the instruments are inlaïd with silver. Inscriptions mention oculists from other provinces including one from Dalmatia, two from Spain, and a bilingual Graeco-Latin example from Cherchel, North Africa. Several Gallic reliefs may depict oculists, particularly a scene from Montiers-sur-Saulx (Meuse) where the doctor is examining a woman's eyes.

Healing was closely bound up with religion. The second-century orator Aelius Aristides, born in Asia Minor, wrote a diary about the various illnesses which plagued him for over 12 years. Asthma, catarrh, headache, hypertension, insomnia and various internal troubles have all been identified and were not much alleviated by the treatments advised by various doctors. Aristides got more help from his dreams and visions of Asclepius,

28 Surgeon's equipment. Bingen

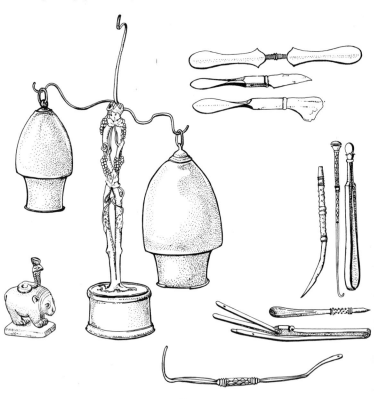

the Greek god of healing (with shrines at Epidaurus, Pergamum, Cos etc. About 292 B.C. after a plague, the cult in the form of a sacred snake was brought to Rome and a temple built). After turning to Asclepius as his medical adviser, Aristides gradually let the god take over his life as his guide and the inspiration of his work, and this close relationship brought him much comfort.

Inscriptions, literary references and reliefs suggest that either the sick in search of healing or their relatives prayed to the god. If this was not sufficient they went to the nearest temple, purified themselves by bathing, and offered a simple sacrifice of cakes, figs, or baked meat. They then spent the night in the temple or an adjacent building and dreamt or believed they saw a vision of the god as a kindly bearded man or a beautiful youth. The patient discussed his disease with the god and was healed or else was advised to take certain remedies; swim in the sea or bathe in a spring, ride and take exercise, take part in religious ceremonies, diet, or divert his mind by composing poetry or comic mimes for the stage. The prescriptions seem to have been clear and very individual, if sometimes surprising to the patient. They were not always efficacious nor were all patients as successful dreamers as Aristides, but inscriptions testify to many cures and even the physician Galen acted on advice received in dreams. There is no evidence that Asclepius's priests acted as his intermediaries. His success is difficult to explain. Some of it may have been due to auto-suggestion; some of it due to the patients' acquaintance with medical knowledge of the period; while the atmosphere of the temple inspired their dreams.

Once established in Rome, the Romans took Asclepius, under his Latin name of Aesculapius, to their hearts. The army introduced his cult in the most distant corners of the Empire and dedications to him are found on the frontiers as well as in the cities. His worship was supported by the wealthier patients, the poor were treated free. The lodgings provided for the sick at his major temples were probably the first religious hospitals. One grew up round Aesculapius's shrine on an island in the Tiber at Rome, and others may have existed in other cities. The army soon built hospitals for the sick and wounded, usually ranges of small rooms separated by a corridor built round a courtyard or garden in the quieter part of the fort. Other rooms acted as operating theatres and stores. Fine examples are known from fortresses such as Neuss, Xanten or Windisch. At Aquincum a stamp impressed on a wooden wine-barrel showed that wine for the hospital was duty-free.

Numerous deities were associated with water and all over the Empire the sick sought relief at healing springs. Many modern spas indeed may be said to have originated in this way, among them Baden Baden where Caracalla decorated the baths with marble as a thank offering after obtaining relief from his rheumatism; or the spring and temple dedicated to the British goddess Sulis and the Roman Minerva at Bath. The worship of Roman deities concerned with healing is often combined with local cults in this fashion. The Spanish silver cup(72) depicts a nymph, Salus of Umeri, with her spring from which boys are

29   *Votive offerings from the sanctuary at the source of the Seine, Dijon,* a, *wood.* b–d, *stone*

filling jars and pouring the water into a cask on a cart. On the right a sick man sitting in a wicker chair is being offered a drink. On the left the same man, recovered, makes a thank offering.

Most interesting among recent discoveries are those made at the source of the Seine near Dijon, presided over by the goddess Sequana. In a large pool 190 carved wooden objects were found, statuettes, heads, limbs or other pieces of human anatomy, some crudely carved, others, like the woman's head (*29a*), far more elegant work. They probably represent the offerings of pilgrims seeking a cure at a Gaulish sanctuary. When the cult developed on Roman lines in the first century A.D. two temples were built with accommodation for priests and pilgrims and a ritual bathing pool. Stone votive offerings replace wood, including figures bringing gifts of money, animals, or fruit. It has been possible to identify some diseases from the sculpture. Limbs show fractures, rheumatism and gout, and there is a foot with a sponge soaked in sacred water fixed to the Achilles tendon (*29c*) and a child's leg with a metal support. The list includes bandaged hernias, leprosy, breast cancer, and mental deficiency. Cooling compresses sooth neuralgia (*29d*) and closed eyes denote blindness (*29b*).

GAMES OF CHANCE

If suitable recreation formed part of medical treatment, the healthy also willingly shared in it. Gambling, in spite of unsuccessful laws to curb it, was a favourite pastime. Bets were made on a variety of events and games were played with the familiar six-sided dice. Games boards often occur scratched on steps in public places, and beautiful inlaid gaming tables have been described by Martial and other authors. For one game known as *Duodecim Scripta* each player had 15 pieces, and three dice were thrown to determine each move. *Latrunculi* (soldiers or brigands) was a complicated war game using pieces of different colours with various moves. A Trier relief shows a game in progress. Ausonius ascribes a prodigious memory for every move in these games to the orator Minervius, one of the Bordeaux professors, and an inscription from Aquitaine mentions a schoolmaster as a keen player of *Latrunculi*. From Timgad comes evidence for Three Men's Morris, perhaps a development of noughts and crosses, the object of which was to get three pieces in a row.

MUSIC

Music is known to have played a considerable part in Roman life. The Greek influence was strong and many of the performers were Greeks. Oriental influences were also important. Of the more local contributions of Etruscan, Celtic or Teutonic origin we hear little, but they must have existed. We know that solo singers and choirs were essential features of religious festivals and dramatic performances, that under the Romans the simple instrumental accompaniments of the Greeks developed into huge orchestras, and the eminent soloists received excessive adulation, went on concert tours, and had statues put up in their honour. Amateur talent was also fostered as an accomplishment. Singing was good for declamation and both boys and girls might have lessons in dancing and playing the cithara. Musical slaves were cherished and at times the homes of the well-to-do seem to have reverberated with their practising.

Amateurs may have still used the lyre with its tortoiseshell soundbox, but usually it was replaced by the cithara with a broad wood soundbox extending up into the two wood sidepieces which helped to amplify the sound. One appears on the side of the sarcophagus of Julia Tyrrania at Arles(*30*). It could have up to eleven strings looped around bone pegs for tuning, and was usually played with a plectrum. It varied in size, Seneca describes with disgust concert citharas as large as litters. Small harps and lutes were also played, often by Oriental slave girls. The tombstone of the 16-year-old Lutatia Lupata, a foster child at Merida, shows her fingering a stringed instrument.

Wind instruments are represented by the aulos, really a whole family of pipes with a cylindrical bore, reed-blown, with single or double reeds. Their nearest modern equivalents are the clarinet and oboe, and actual examples made of wood, ivory or bronze have been found at Pompeii and in Egypt. They were often played in pairs, kept in position by inserting them in the mouth through holes cut in a leather band which went round the musician's head. His cheeks acted as bellows as he blew. The end of one pipe often curved upwards. Such a pair appear clearly on a Cologne mosaic with a maenad giving a lively performance(*31*). Here the keying arrangements for blocking different sound-holes and altering the pitch appear clearly.

Simpler bone pipes and whistles could be heard in rural areas and a number have been found in the Rhineland. A bronze

30   Coffin of Julia Tyrrania. Arles

31   Detail. Dionysus mosaic, Cologne. Satyr and maenad

whistle from Mainz has a mouthpiece inserted in the back of a statuette of a hooded man, the air escaping through a gap in his cloak(*37a*). The syrinx or pan-pipes was also a favourite companion of shepherds, as well as occurring frequently in a religious context. One is just visible on Julia Tyrrania's coffin(*30*). Actual examples made of box-wood have been found in wells at Alesia and Barbing-Kreuzhof (Bavaria). Percussion instruments included cymbals, small drums, and tambourines.

At the other extreme from the pipings of the countryside was the *hydraulis*, the water organ, so-called because air was blown into a chamber containing an inverted metal bowl immersed in water. The balance between air and water forced surplus air into pipes which were opened by moving slides. The instrument is depicted on a clay model from Carthage, several gems and pottery fragments, on Julia Tyrrania's coffin(*30*), and on mosaics from Nennig, Hama in Syria, and Zliten(*32*). At Aquincum the organ, destroyed by fire in the third century, has been reconstructed as the bronze pipes, originally arranged in four rows, and other material survived among the ashes (see p. 125).

The organ was an important item of the Roman orchestra for accompanying chorus and dancers. The Zliten mosaic shows part of the amphitheatre band with the tuba or straight trumpet, possibly an Etruscan invention, and the cornu, a trumpet curved into the shape of a G held by a wooden cross-bar(*32*). A Roman inscription refers to a Guild of Bandsmen who performed at public rituals, otherwise such instruments really belong with the army which used them for signalling and enlivening parades. The carnyx, a curved trumpet with its bell-shaped end replaced by a fierce dragon's head, is well known among the reliefs of fighting Gauls on the triumphal arch at Orange.

32 Mosaic. The amphi-theatre band and two gladiators. Zliten

HUNTING AND FISHING

Hunting for sport or fitness as well as for food was a favourite Roman pastime, and fishing was also enjoyed. Ausonius wrote to his friend Theon, who lived on the Atlantic coast in Médoc, inciting him to write poetry but imagining him otherwise engaged in trading, chasing thieves or cattle raiders (or perhaps sharing their spoils), or else surrounded with fishing nets, hooks and lines in a house overflowing with sturgeon, tunnyfish, stingray and plaice. Or was he hunting deer or wild boar in the forest, undeterred by the ugly scars displayed by his brother? The same author also describes river fish from the Moselle: salmon, perch and eels etc. Fishermen appear not infrequently on North African mosaics such as the one from Althiburos (see p. 169).

Partridges lured by a decoy and an encounter with a wild boar are among the scenes on the Oudna mosaic (53), and another panel from the same villa shows three hunters and the dogs Ederatus (ivy-crowned) and Mustela (weasel) in hot pursuit of a hare and a fox (33). Hunters rejoiced in their successes, soldiers in particular making the most of their opportunities. In Germany an army officer put up an altar to Diana to celebrate a bag of 50 bears in six months. And on the Yorkshire moors Gaius Micianus, a cavalry commander, gladly dedicated an altar to Silvanus after capturing a boar of remarkable fineness which many of his predecessors had failed to bag.

The capture of animals for the *Venatio*, the wild beast hunt in the amphitheatre in which men fought animals or animals fought each other, developed into a large-scale trading enterprise. Mosaics from the Sicilian villa of Piazza Armerina show a variety of creatures being driven into nets and enclosures and then caged ready for transport by cart and ship. Many of the animals came from Africa and a villa mosaic from Bône in Algeria shows the capture of ostriches, antelopes, Barbary sheep, lions and leopards.

The games of Rome originated as a thank offering to Jupiter after a victory. In time the association with triumphs ceased, and games in honour of various deities were regularly given by magistrates or priests taking up office, and by emperors on various occasions. By the fourth century A.D. 177 days annually might be devoted to them. The games were chiefly chariot races or theatrical performances. Gladiatorial contests and fights between wild beasts never played an important part. These

33   Mosaic depicting a hare hunt. Oudna

activities formed part of special shows which were given far less frequently.

THEATRES AND AMPHITHEATRES

Roman theatres comprised an auditorium, or *cavea*, with seats ranged in tiers to a considerable height, built round a horseshoe-shaped curve. This enclosed the orchestra a flat arena with seats for the important members of the audience – not musicians. The seats were reached through vaulted corridors and a covered-in colonnade above the upper tiers. The stage was raised in front of an elaborate façade with doorways, columns, niches and other architectural embellishments. The stage building was roofed, and canvas awnings fixed on masts above the top tiers of seats protected many of the audience from sun or rain.

Many Roman stone theatres survive and in the eastern provinces they often succeeded earlier Greek ones. A good example of a Roman stage building can be seen at Sabratha, one of the largest theatres in North Africa, dating from the late second century(*34*). It is decorated with 108 Corinthian columns originally of marble or granite which are arranged in three storeys and covered with a coffered wooden ceiling. Projecting wings and rooms at the back of the stage were used as green-rooms. Marble reliefs attached to the front of the stage depicted the Muses, masks, and scenes from mime and pantomime. A stage curtain was used which descended into a long narrow pit when the performance began.

34   Aerial view of the theatre, Sabratha, with the elaborate stage setting

The same arrangement for lowering the curtain, a Roman innovation controlled by a system of weights, was found at Lyons where the theatre built during the reign of Augustus was extended to hold 10,700 people under Hadrian. Next to it is the odeum which held 3,000, and was intended for musical contests, lectures or recitations. Much of it was roofed, light being admitted by a semicircular space left open above the orchestra(*35*). The orchestra floors in both theatre and odeum were covered with slabs of different coloured marbles – green, pink and grey.

The wild beast shows and gladiatorial battles took place in the amphitheatres, buildings with tiers of seats built round a central arena, protected by a high wall so that the animals could not escape among the spectators(*36*). Many cities had both theatres and amphitheatres, the latter were also particularly popular in Gaul. The army used them for exercises and parades as well as for entertainment so amphitheatres are also found near fortresses and frontier towns. In northern Gaul and Britain more economical buildings which combined the functions of both theatre and amphitheatre were developed. In the eastern provinces theatres were also converted for amphitheatre sports. At Corinth in the

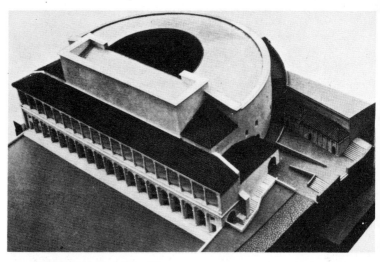

35 *Reconstruction. The odeum, Lyons*

36 *The amphitheatre. El Djem*

early third century the stage and the front row of seats were cut back to make room for an arena which, at a still later date, was turned into a tank for aquatic displays.

Theatrical performances

In contrast to the dramatic output of earlier times, the Roman Empire produced few playwrights. Revivals of both Greek and Latin plays were not uncommon especially in the east, but one cannot be sure whether complete plays or only isolated scenes were performed. Popular taste was for increasingly sensational entertainment with fine costumes and parades of actors and animals. Myths or historic themes were often mimed by dancers, one soloist playing several parts wearing an assortment of different masks. The story was told by solo singers or a choir accompanied by the aulos, cithara or an orchestra. Apuleius describes a dance in the Corinth theatre with Venus surrounded by Cupids and Graces, and Minerva with demons. The scene was Mount Ida and at the end it descended below the stage on a hoist. The audience were very vocal and the best dancers were adored. Pylades, a Cilician and Augustus's freedman, wrote a book on pantomime and his work was long remembered in the ballet schools. Sidonius Apollinaris in the fifth century describes the entertainments given by his friend Consentius: Caramallus and Phabaton with gestures of legs, knees, arms and the whole body depicted in pantomime such scenes as Medea and Jason, Jupiter as the bull or the swan deceiving Europa or Leda, Ganymede, Perseus and Andromeda, or the Trojan war.

Most popular of all were the mime plays, scenes from everyday life with topical jokes and horseplay or disrespectful portrayals of the Olympian gods, enlivened by dancing girls and variety turns including jugglers and tightrope walkers. Bronze statuettes of a dancing negro from Carnuntum and an acrobat and a snake charmer from Autun probably depict some of these per-formers (*37b, c*). The Atellan farce, an entertainment orig-inating in pre-Roman Italy, used stock characters such as the glutton, the hunchback, the old man, or a spook called Lamia. It became popular chiefly in the western provinces and terracotta masks worn by the actors have been found in Germany (*37e*).

Actors might be either slaves or freedmen, usually viewed with disdain by their audiences with the exception of the popular stars who sometimes became respected citizens. Various honours were showered on imperial favourites. Some wealthy men owned troupes of actors, among them Valerius Asiaticus of Vienne in the first century. Touring companies travelled from city to city to take part in the contests and performances of the various games.

95

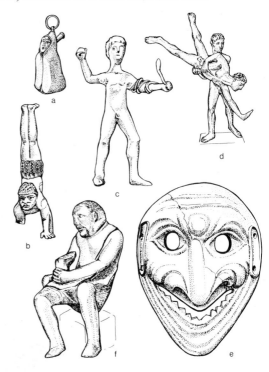

37 *Bronze statuettes,*
a, *whistle, Mainz.*
b, *acrobat, Autun.*
c, *snake-charmer, and*
d, *wrestlers. Musée des*
antiquités nationales.
e, *pottery mask, Worms.*
f, *cobbler, Rheims*

Gladiatorial contests

Gladiatorial fighting was an Etruscan practice originally closely bound up with religion and funeral observances. Men fought to the death by the tomb of a chief to strengthen his spirit with a blood sacrifice. The Roman nobility put on exhibitions of fighting in memory of their eminent dead, but by Caesar's time these had turned into public entertainments. The gladiators were usually criminals, slaves or prisoners of war; but some free men, who either enjoyed fighting or were short of money, also contracted themselves to the gladiatorial schools. Training schools are known to have existed in many cities including Alexandria, Pergamum and Autun.

The gladiators were divided into several groups including the heavily-armed men, the 'Mirmillones', who wore helmets decorated with a fish; the lightly-armed 'Thracians' with light shield and scimitar and the 'Retiarii' who carried only a net, long trident and dagger. They relied on their agility to exhaust their opponents. Some skilful fighters survived many combats. An

Asiatic at Orange won 53 fights and a 25-year-old Greek killed at Nîmes and a 35-year-old Romanian at Cadiz, had already gained 20 victories. At Vienne a 'Thracian' has seven crowns and two crossed palm branches on his tombstone denoting 17 successes. Some survivors won the wooden sword of retirement and stayed on as instructors.

Numerous discoveries of statuettes, reliefs, mosaics, glass and pottery depicting gladiators reflect the popularity of such sport. This is echoed by graffiti such as the 'Retiarius' Herculanus depicted at Apulum(*38*). Another Retiarius in action is depicted on a mosaic from the villa at Nennig; the figure of the trainer appears in the background superintending the battle.

Other amphitheatre sports included wrestling, depicted on a mosaic from Aquincum, where one man has seized the other in a body hold, or by a bronze statuette from Gaul(*37d*), and boxing. The heavy Roman leather boxing gloves were sometimes weighted or spiked with metal causing fatal results – as the wife of Apollonius tells us on his tombstone at Nicomedia, Bithynia, which was paid for from his winnings. Apollonius was eight times victorious, but met his end in his ninth boxing match. At Barcelona a retired centurion left 7,500 denarii to the city to be invested at six per cent and the interest used to finance an annual boxing match and oil for the public baths.

Instead of fighting gladiators the animals might be trained to entertain, and a mosaic from Rades (Tunisia) shows a troupe of performing bears, all with names: one, Fedra, is climbing a pole while the others are sporting with bulls, boars, and birds.

38   Graffito of the gladiator Herculanus, Apulum

97

CHARIOT RACES

Chariot racing was a passion for all classes throughout the Empire. There was keen rivalry between the Reds, Whites, Blues and Greens. In Rome each of these factions had its own organization to find the best horses and drivers. In the provinces presumably similar, smaller organizations or agents supplied these requisites.

The circus or hippodrome had two long parallel sides and one rounded end all lined with seats for the spectators. The other end was filled with stables and the starting boxes for the teams. A central rib, the spina, ran down the middle with three pyramids or obelisks at each end. One of these survives from the circus at Vienne, others are visible on a glass cup from Colchester(*80*). Each race consisted of several laps counted by placing objects like large eggs on racks in the spina. A mosaic from Lyons shows a race in progress: two teams have come to grief through turning the corners too sharply; men on foot are ready to cut the charioteer free from the reins after a crash, or to throw water on the wheels which tended to smoulder.

The chariot race was a favourite motif for decoration. The series of glass cups found in the western provinces and probably made in northern Italy often have the names of famous charioteers. The Colchester one(*80a*) lists Cresces, Hierax, Olympus, and Antilochus, with Cresces the probable winner. A Tarragona tombstone shows Eutychus holding the victor's palm branch, but he died at 22 and was lamented in verse. Fuscus, perhaps his comrade, was also bewailed with a Latin panegyric and at the end a comment in Greek that future ages shall speak of the exploits of this hero of the Blue faction. A mosaic fragment from Dougga shows the charioteer Eros driving his horses with the victor's wreath, and the starting stalls in the background. Two of the horses are called Amandus (Darling) and Frunitus (Jolly). African horses were among the best and mosaics from Cherchel, Sousse and Constantine show them off duty.

ATHLETICS

In addition to theatre, amphitheatre and circus, some cities also had a stadium for athletics. Lyons probably possessed all four as well as the odeum. In plan the stadium resembled the circus but without the stables and central spina. A well-preserved example survives at Aphrodisias which is 263 m. (855 ft) long and held audiences of up to 30,000.

In Greece traditional games of this sort continued at four-year intervals in the great religious centres. Competitions for singing, for instrumental music, original poems and declamations formed part of the games. Prizes were often a laurel or parsley wreath and the title of victor, but inscriptions from Aphrodisias list money awards ranging from 2,700 denarii for the best tragic actor to 150 for the top boy lyre player. The athletic contests had different classes for men, youths and boys. An inscription has been found at Tyre commemorating Eutyches of Ephesus, winner of the Pentathlon (pitching the quoit, running, jumping, hurling and wrestling) at the Heraclian games.

5

Industry and natural resources

COMMERCE

The identification of at least 119 shops in one area of Volubilis is a reminder of the busy commercial life of Roman towns and, as we have seen, the provision of shops featured not infrequently in the gifts and bequests of citizens. The shopkeepers must have obtained their supplies in various ways. Perishable foodstuffs would be grown in the market gardens, sometimes within the city boundaries, but more often outside the walls and brought in by carts and pack animals. Cereals and heavier requisites like timber and building material arrived by wagon at Volubilis, and provision for wagon-parking was found at a number of houses. Wherever a suitable river or harbour made it possible, ships and barges were also used.

Businessmen constructed store-houses to receive such loads, and a row of large vaulted rooms serving this purpose was found on a terrace below the agora at Tomi on the western shore of the Black Sea. In them were 100 amphorae containing resin, dyes, bitumen etc., iron ingots and anchors, candlesticks, and seven large weights, as well as the head of a bronze statue. Shopkeepers, no doubt, bought in smaller quantities from such stores. The right to hold a market every eight days was a cherished privilege. Eventually the Roman world adopted the seven-day week so that markets fell on different days and neighbouring towns had to avoid clashing with each other. In the country permission was also granted for markets in non-urban areas and on the imperial estates.

Literary sources and inscriptions provide evidence for commercial life. For example from the Syrian city of Dura-Europos, occupied by the Romans from A.D. 165 until 256, come allusions to the sale of food such as meat, bread, honey and honey-cakes, vegetables, fresh and dried fish, cheese, salt, caraway and cummin, wax, firewood and drinking water, perfumes, women's hair, drugs, wool, textiles, pottery, glass, jewellery, metal objects, boots, slaves, and landed property such as houses, fields or vineyards. One account lists the purchase of barley, oil, meat and wine, and also 40 denarii for self, presumably personal pocket-money. Sometimes people selling the same product lived in the same area. Jerusalem is known to have had a wool-traders' quarter, Ephesus a 'place for the bread-mixers' and Cyrene a street of perfume sellers. Often however, shops selling various wares existed side by side and businesses which needed working quarters, such as bakeries and fulleries, sometimes used parts of the adjacent houses.

SHOPS

The clearest impression of small Roman shops is obtained from the examples surviving at Pompeii, but in addition to sites such as Vaison (see p. 53), we have from France a fine series of stone reliefs depicting shops, put up as part of imposing funeral monuments by rich tradesmen. The shopkeeper usually sits on a high-backed chair or solid stool behind a counter, like the one from Metz(39), a scene in a patisserie. The customer is pointing at some of the small cakes and sweets strung together which are

39
The Patisserie,
Metz

stacked on the shelves, with larger cakes or loaves on the counter.
A scene from Dijon shows a wine-seller dispensing local products
at a counter probably built out over a colonnaded street(*40*). A
customer holds up a jug which is filled through a pipe; a row of six
more jugs may be measures. The wine was probably kept in
barrels under the counter and part of a tombstone from Autun
shows a man walking along with a small cask on his shoulder.

The Dijon relief also shows part of a butcher's shop next door
to the wine-seller. Objects hanging up appear to be sausages, and
lying on the counter may be pigs' heads or pieces of bacon. The
large barrel in the foreground may contain lard. A Narbonne
inscription mentions a *lardarius* and Gaul was famous for hams.
Strabo comments on the quantities of pork eaten, both fresh and
salted, and the pigs fed on acorns by the Sequani near Dijon
produced highly esteemed delicacies. Spanish hams were also
well known, and those of the Menapii in Belgium were exported
to Italy in large quantities.

Food was not only sold in shops. A stall in the forum or market
appears on one of the Arlon funerary reliefs. Apples and pears are
spread out on a trestle table; in front stand three fruit baskets and
more may be hung up sideways at the back (alternatively the
sculptor may be intending to depict bundles of leeks); a young
assistant watches the stallkeeper try to attract the custom of a
passer-by who feels his wares dubiously. A Bordeaux relief also

shows fruit being offered for
sale in four open sacks, and a
woman with her hand in a
sack of grain. And a Gallo-
Roman street-cry survives on
a fragment found at Nar-
bonne depicting a man with a
basket of apples hung round
his neck by a strap, a fly swat
in his hand, and the words
'apples, ladies'!

40   Wine shop, Dijon

MILLING AND BAKING

A pleasant feature of town life must have been the bakers' shops, and a number of these have been identified at Volubilis. They have corn mills of the Pompeian type with a hollow upper stone of hour-glass shape turning on an iron spindle on a lower conical stone. A wooden beam ran through sockets in the upper stone so that it could be pushed around by men or donkeys. Grain poured in at the top was caught after grinding in a wooden channel or dish at the bottom. The flour was stored in large jars. When it was mixed into dough it was placed in a trough with a series of cross bars and rotating blades which kneaded it mechanically. Then the round loaves were baked in a clay oven with a domed cover, heated with wood or charcoal. The loaves were sold in an adjoining shop. Smaller millstones found in houses show that grain was also ground at home but the absence of ovens suggests that the baking was still done at the bakery.

The hourglass mill with stones preferably of rough and porous volcanic lava has been found elsewhere – in North Africa, Greece, Gaul and Britain. At Narbonne the memorial put up by M. Careieus Asisa, a freedman baker, to members of his family including a six-year-old daughter, shows one of these mills in use propelled by a donkey wearing blinkers(*41*); on the right is a large dog with a bell on its collar. On 9 June the asses or horses

41   Corn mill. Narbonne

who turned the mills had a holiday when the millers celebrated the festival of their patron, the goddess Vesta.

Civilian bakeries have also been found at Aquincum and Emona. Pottery moulds with designs for decorating the cakes baked in them were used: examples have turned up at Aquincum and Poetovio, and in Britain at Silchester. At Carnuntum a cakemaker, Ulpius Vitalis, dedicated an altar to Mithras, but it is not clear whether his cakes were for general consumption or for sacrificial purposes. Athenaeus and other literary sources list various different breads, cakes and other specialities from many towns in Asia Minor including *panem divinum* from Ancyra. Lydian cooks seem to have been particularly famous. The baker's trade was a highly respected one and in Rome, rich baker contractors like Eurysaces reflect the importance of this occupation in large urban centres.

By the end of the first century B.C. the water-driven grain-mill was in use, and Strabo mentions one some miles inland from the Black Sea. Evidence for them has been found in Britain, and Ausonius notes one driven by a tributary of the Moselle although this may have been used to drive marble-cutting saws rather than for grinding grain. To prevent excess profits the Emperor Diocletian published an edict listing maximum permitted prices in A.D. 301. This gave the cost of a water-mill at 2,000 denarii as compared with 1,250 denarii for a donkey-mill and 250 for a small hand-mill.

At Barbégal, three miles from Arles, are the striking remains of a large flour mill where water from an aqueduct was collected in a reservoir and then directed down a slope in two streams which each ran through eight levels arranged in steps. Each level contained a water-wheel turning millstones which could grind three tons of flour in the course of a ten-hour day. This establishment was probably a third-century state enterprise. Some scholars believe that it was planned by A. Candidus Benignus whose stone coffin has been found at Arles, as the inscription refers to his ability as a water engineer and describes him as a member of the guild of carpenters and builders, possessing the greatest skill. 'A modest man, great craftsmen called him master. Sweet-tempered, he knew how to entertain his friends, gentle and studious, his was a kindly spirit.' The woodworker's skill would also have been needed at Barbégal to design the water-wheels and other wooden fittings.

CLOTHES

Much Roman clothing was made of wool, and some Roman fashions spread to the provinces. Reliefs from Italy and other parts of the Empire show people dressed in tunics consisting of two pieces of material sewn together at the sides and at the shoulders, sleeveless or with sleeves of varying length. One or more of these were worn, slightly bloused with a girdle. Women wore ankle-length tunics of similar type.

For official occasions Roman male citizens donned the toga, a large piece of cloth about 6 m. (19½ ft) in length, draped round the body with some of the fullness tucked into a tunic girdle, and one long end thrown over the left shoulder. Although a very dignified garment, its wearer needed skilled help, usually provided by a trained slave, to drape it correctly. It was also heavy and inconvenient to wear, and as time went on it was often replaced by more comfortable fashions.

Diocletian's edict lists some of the linen and woollen garments being bought at that period. Among them are linen shirts, tunics, hoods, loin-cloths, girdles, pocket handkerchiefs and head bands. Most of the linen came from the east Mediterranean provinces, places such as Byblos, Tarsus and Laodicea. Linen factories also existed in Gaul. The woollen goods include a variety of cloaks and tunics for men, women and children. Most interesting is the *byrrus*, a long voluminous cape often with a hood and probably of Gallic origin. One is worn by the customer in a shopping scene from Buzenol, Belgium (*42*). The best were made by the Nervii round Bavai and cost 10,000 denarii. These were imitated at Laodicea, and cheaper ones came from Noricum, Dacia, Britain and Malta, with the North African product, at 3,000 denarii, the cheapest of all. The *paenula*, a less well-fitting cape usually worn

42   Sale of cloth, Buzenol

with a scarf, had a maximum price of 5,000 denarii for those made at Laodicea, and the heavy rectangular *sagum*, which could be used as a blanket, cost up to 8,000. The fringed Gallic *sagum* became particularly popular in Italy and, indeed, quantities of wearing apparel for export were eventually produced in Gaul. The cloth for the *byrrus* and *paenula* was probably woven in a semicircular piece, or in segments later stitched together. The prices given may only be for the material, and charges for making up and for dyeing if required, would have to be added.

Other articles of native dress tended to survive in Gaul. Many reliefs from France and Germany show both sexes wearing a very wide tunic, ungirt and with or without wide sleeves. Men wore it to just below the knee, women to ankle length. It is known as the Gallic coat and an actual example has survived in a German bog. It was woven in one piece starting at the outer edge of one sleeve; the width being increased for the body and decreased for the second sleeve. A hole was cut for the head and ornamental stitching added round the neck. The seams for the sides and the sleeves were sewn up, and some material was turned in to make narrower cuffs. A woman's dress, however, found in a grave at Les-Martres-de-Veyre, was made of a single piece of material seamed on one side with the seams set in separately. Probably the extra length made it impossible to combine the two. A statue from Wintersdorf on the Sauer depicts a man wearing a sleeveless Gallic coat on his way to the baths with towels, strigil and oilflask, and the ship merchant Blussus also wears it under a cape(*74* and see p. 168).

Women usually had the Gallic coat with a rectangular cloak worn like a stole or over one shoulder, and sometimes drawn over the head. Blussus's wife Menimane, however, wears a close-fitting bodice with long tight sleeves ending in cuffs, and a front opening fastened with a large brooch. Over this she wore a tunic pinned on each shoulder by brooches and to the front of the bodice by another brooch; the fold on the left shoulder has slipped down over her arm. The tunic is fringed round the hem. A cloak draped over the right shoulder was also secured there by a brooch.

FULLERS AND CLOTH-MAKING

In cities it was customary to send out the togas, cloaks and other large items of wearing apparel to the fullers' shops for laundering. The clothes were placed in tubs full of water, soda or other alkaline substances, and trodden on until they were clean. They were dried and bleached on a frame placed over a pot of burning sulphur and then straightened out in a large clothes' press. Pompeii has produced several recognizable fuller's shops as well as paintings showing the work being carried on. Similar facilities must have existed in provincial cities, and a relief from Sens shows a fuller at work. At Alzey in Upper Germany another fuller, Vitalinus Secundinus, set up an altar to Minerva, the patron goddess of his trade. At Sasemon in Spain a tablet is put up to an illustrious human patron by a list of dedicators who include two fullers, one shoemaker, and a nailsmith; most on the list are freedmen but one at least is a slave.

The fullers were also concerned with the finishing processes for newly-woven cloth. While spinning and some weaving and clothes-making for domestic purposes was done at home, textiles were also produced for sale in the shops. The products of the looms in houses or small weaving establishments came to the fullers for washing, beating with mallets to give a closer texture and combing to raise the nap. The nap was then trimmed, and another Sens relief shows a fuller using a large pair of shears for this purpose. The actual implements have been found at Great Chesterford, Britain, and at the Hungarian villa of Balacza on Lake Balaton. After bleaching and pressing, the new cloth was ready for use or, if the thread had not been dyed in the fleece, it might be sent to a dye works. Two of these were found at Pompeii with glass bottles containing traces of the various colours, and stone or metal vats set over a furnace. Old clothes could also be redipped or dyed different colours.

Textile fragments of Roman date are sometimes preserved in the dry conditions of provinces in the Near East, notably at Palmyra and Dura Europos; and by the damp conditions provided by wells in the west. Many have been found with burials and mostly comprise scraps of protective coverings such as shrouds. Current research is producing fresh information about details of manufacture. It appears that in the western provinces yarn of wool, linen, or hemp was spun with the spindle rotating clockwise, while in the east it was twirled in the opposite direction. These differences go back to pre-Roman times and show that the two great textile areas of the Empire in northern Gaul and the Levant continued independently to follow their own traditions. Most of the material recovered is in plain weave or the stronger twill, but more elaborate fancy weaves appear in the third century, probably as a result of experiments in Syria. Wall-paintings show colourful clothes and soft-furnishings; garments might have woven bands, and tartan seems to have been a Gaulish invention. The most luxurious attire was dyed with a purple made from shellfish found along the Syrian coast: Tyre was famous for the dye.

The sale of cloth or completed garments appears on a number of grave reliefs. The Secundinii who put up the Igel column near Trier were a rich family of wool merchants and on their monument there is one scene in which a piece of cloth is being displayed to a prospective customer, and a record being made of the transaction. At Buzenol, buyer and seller are regarding some cloth with unusual approval(*42*) and an unopened bale, still corded up, is on the ground between them, while at Herzweiler near Trier a piece with a fringe is being inspected for flaws. One of the Sens reliefs shows the hands and scissors of a tailor cutting cloth on a counter. Several hoods ready for sale hang from a rail above him. A Trier relief depicts what may be a store with rolls of cloth piled up on high shelves above either cloth or clothing hanging on pegs. For transport cloth was packed into large bales and a Neumagen relief shows a stalwart individual in a leather apron weighing one.

HEADGEAR

Some Gallic ladies wore hair nets or bonnets of thin material fitting closely over their hair. The married women of the Ubii who lived round Cologne, however, wore an immense bonnet supported by interior cross-strings fastened with a tag on one cheek. This appears in an exaggerated form on reliefs of the local mother goddesses(*89* and p. 192). In Noricum and Pannonia prevalent local fashions include female head coverings of soft round caps, sometimes worn with a veil, or large fur hats. Some high round hats have veils draped to fall down at the back like wimples. A charming relief of a Norican girl from Klagenfurt shows a tight long-sleeved ankle-length tunic below a sleeveless dress tucked up at the knee(*43*) with the typical large local brooches holding it in position on the shoulder(*46e*). A piece of jewellery is suspended from her girdle, and she carries a mirror and a jewel box. Fringed aprons were also worn by some Norican women.

43   *Norican girl, Klagenfurt*

LEG COVERINGS

Comparatively little is known of coverings for the legs. Roman soldiers wore leather breeches, but trousers otherwise were only worn by barbarians. Leggings of puttee type were sometimes used, and the woman's burial at Les-Martres-de-Veyre produced stockings of wool fabric. Men on the Sens and Neumagen reliefs appear to be wearing socks, probably with a separate division for the big toe, as well as sandals. Leather shoes survive frequently in very dry or damp surroundings. They range from sandals or delicate slippers of supple leather dyed in various colours and sometimes with the uppers cut out in various designs, to bootees with leather or cloth uppers completely covering the foot. Substantial boots and sandals with single or double soles, often nail-studded, were worn by soldiers and farm-workers. Reliefs and inscriptions concerned with cobblers are not infrequent. Peregrinus, the Dacian slave of Q. Asinius, who died aged 20, spent his short life making soldiers' boots at Aquincum, and other shoe-makers are commemorated by tombstones from Spain and Asia Minor, sometimes as specialists in certain types of shoes such as sandals or slippers. A well-known relief from Rheims shows a shoe-maker at work astride his bench: well-shod himself, a new shoe is taking shape on a last in front of him; pieces of leather or more shoes appear in a basket under the bench, and tools in a rack on the wall. A less well-preserved relief from Sens depicts a similar scene, but it has been suggested that here wooden rather than leather shoes are being made. Iron lasts of Roman date are found not infrequently, and a Gallic bronze statuette shows a shoe-maker wearing a leather apron holding one(*37f*).

CRAFTS
Carpentry
Timber and stone were important raw materials for all Roman building activities and wood was also needed for boats, furniture, various implements, pit-props and fuel. From Gaul came several portraits of carpenters like the freedman Caius from Bordeaux who holds a rule in one hand and an adze-hammer in the other(*44*). Tools and a couch-end on his tombstone in the Louvre confirm that P. Beitenos, the Greek, was a furniture maker, and Maximus, a freedman from Bithynia, is recorded as a wood-working house-builder of unrivalled skill.

Measuring tools such as rules, dividers, set-squares and levels are also prominent on Roman tombstones. The iron tools survive on excavated sites and are little different from those in use today. Some of them are illustrated on a painted fragment of glass now in the Vatican museum(*45*). A frame-saw appears at *a*, *b* shows a block being trimmed with an axe or adze, *c* shows a bow-drill, *d* a mortice-chisel in use with the patron goddess Minerva looking on; *e* has a plane and at *f*, a shipwright is at work with a large axe. For saws the Romans introduced several innovations, notably the important one of setting the teeth so that they projected right and left alternately and the saw could be pushed as well as pulled. The frame-saw with the blade fixed between the wooden uprights connected by a crossbar(*45a*) also developed in various sizes; the larger ones could be used for double-sawing with one workman standing above the other on trestles, as on a relief from Nancy. The plane is particularly interesting: it may have been a Greek invention and the Elder Pliny is well acquainted with it; it consisted of a narrow blade wedged at an angle so that it protruded through the iron sole of a box-like wooden body; the iron portions are sometimes found and fragments have come from over 60 British, Gallic, German and Swiss sites. Even the beechwood portions of a plane survived in a well in the Saalburg fort, and a relief from this site shows a man using a plane.

44 *Carpenter, Bordeaux*

45 *Fragment of painted glass, Rome, showing carpenters at work with various tools.* a, *frame saw.* b, *axe or adze.* c, *bow drill.* d, *mortice chisel.* e, *plane.* f, *axe.*

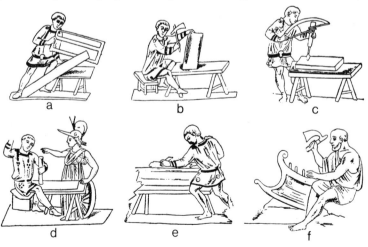

Gaius, son of Getulus, appears on his tombstone at Autun holding a rule, a trowel and a hammer, and accompanied by a frame-saw and an axe-adze. As the frame-saw was also used for stone cutting it is possible that he was a builder or mason rather than a carpenter. Inscriptions mentioning a stone mason or marble cutter are known from Arles, Narbonne, Nîmes and Trier, and Trier also had a stone coffin maker.

Jewellery

Many towns have produced evidence for metal-working in the forms of hearths, slag, and scraps of metal or crucibles. With the brooch as an essential item of dress, the shops selling jewellery were very necessary, and the *aurifex* or goldsmith was an honoured craftsman. Tombstones such as the one of Blussus and his wife(*74*), or the splendid reliefs of Palmyrene ladies show the liveliness of the market, and the jewel-box makes frequent appearances in Roman sculpture.

Alexandria and Antioch were important production centres. Decoration was chiselled on plain gold surfaces and from the third century onwards the fine gold fretwork known as *opus interrasile* appears. Precious stones including sapphires, emeralds or plasma, aquamarines, topaz, garnet, cornelian, occasional uncut diamonds and pearls were used in bezel settings for rings, necklaces and bracelets. Gold coins with emperors' portraits appear on rings and pendants used as a gesture of loyalty or perhaps presented as a mark of distinction. Signet rings were important and widely used to seal documents. Engraved gems were popular. A gold ring from Sussex has a nicolo intaglio depicting a figure of Mercury(*46b*). Cameos were also fashionable and were made by carving the weathered surface of a gem or pebble in relief, leaving the rest of the stone as a dark background. One found in a tomb at Patras has a sardonyx cameo of a head of Medusa. A craft centre for cutting cameos is known from Romula in Romania. A late fourth-century betrothal ring with a filigree hoop was found at Richborough in Kent(*46a*), and one from Amiens is engraved '*parvum te amo*', 'I love thee too little'. These are all gold rings. Silver, bronze, and sometimes iron, lead or glass were also used and both men and women usually wore several rings. Some have a small key attached. An altar at Cologne was dedicated by Fatalis, freedman of Laetius Gratus, a dealer in rings.

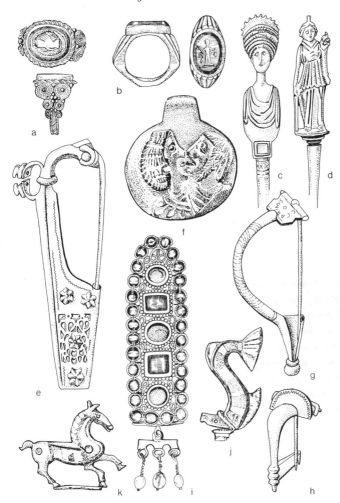

46 Jewellery. a, *gold ring, Richborough.* b, *gold ring, Sussex.* c, *bone pin. British
Museum.* d, *Silver pin, London.* e, *Norican brooch, Vienna.* f, *jet pendant, Chesterholm.*
g, *bronze brooch, Sziszekal.* h, *bronze knee-brooch, Oszony.* i, *gold hair-ornament,
Tunis.* j, k, *bronze enamelled brooches, Oszony*

Several inscriptions found in Spain record the jewellery
decorating statues which women dedicated to the goddess Isis.
The list includes diadems, earrings ornamented with pearls and
other precious stones, necklaces and armlets. At Smyrna the
guild of jewellers and silversmiths also recorded that they had
repaired a statue of Athene which may have been of silver.

In Lyons in 1844 a lucky find revealed a coin hoard buried with the contents of a lady's jewel casket. It includes three pairs of gold bracelets, one pair decorated with a medallion of the Emperor Commodus, another with a head in relief, probably of an empress, and a pair made of twisted strands of gold wire(*47a,d*). Two pairs of earrings consisted of either an emerald, ruby and sapphire strung on a fine gold chain, or a garnet with a gold bar and emerald and pearl pendants (*47 b,c*). Seven necklaces were made up of gold beads(*47e*) or of precious stones and gold leaves or other motifs. One, 29 cm (11 in.) long is of small sapphires(*47g*), another was of blue glass beads imitating lapis-lazuli,(*47h*), and a third is of garnets with a gold fastening and pendant garnets on small gold rings(*47i*). A double chain of coral, gold and malachite with gold spacers 113 cm. (44 in.) long may be a necklace, girdle, or used in hair-dressing as may a strip of gold filigree with a garnet and two emerald pendants at one end.

47   *Jewellery from a woman's grave, Lyons, found 1844*

Jewellery in the east is well represented on Palmyrene tombstones and these show a growing elaboration as Roman peace and security brought increasing prosperity to the cross-desert trade. The portrait of 'Aha, daughter of Halafta', is dated to A.D. 161 (*48*), and shows her wearing three necklaces. One is of small beads or pearls, next come oval and cylindrical beads, and then a necklace of plaited gold and silver wire with an oval pendant with beaded border, a central jewel, and three more jewels suspended from it. An unusual star-shaped brooch, also with pendants, silver or gold bracelets of twisted wire, and earrings similar to the ones found at Lyons also appear. On Aha's right hand is a ring of gold filigree. Other Palmyrene ladies wear as many as seven necklaces and most have tiaras and other hair-decorations. A gold ornament found at Tunis illustrates these fashions: studded with plasma and other stones now lost, it has a pearl border and a pendant of pearls and a sapphire (*46i*). With it was found a bracelet with a central disc inlaid with plasma, sapphires and pearls on an openwork band consisting of gold ivy leaves threaded with pearls. A gold mounted sardonyx cameo brooch depicting the birth of Dionysus, comes from the same site.

The elaborate hairstyles encouraged the production of hair-pins of gold, silver, bone or ivory, carved into busts or small figures or with jewelled heads (*46c,d*). Bronze or bone were used by less wealthy people with necklaces of beads or amber or glass of many colours, and bronze bracelets, some decorated with snakes' heads. Brooches are chiefly found in the western provinces where they developed from earlier Celtic fashions. Simple safety-pin types occur and also specimens set with glass or gems. In the second century enamelled decoration was popular in the western provinces, small fish, insects and animals being great favourites as well as polychrome blobs and discs (*46j,k*). This taste for enamelling gradually spread east along the Rhine-Danube frontier. Near Trier a workshop has been identified in the village of Pachten; here a rectangular hut built on stone foundations was surrounded by a verandah, and a covered way led to a little smelting oven. Copper from nearby deposits had been used for making bronze for brooches and for repairs to metal vessels. A more surprising feature was a number of coin-moulds: similar moulds are known from other sites but bare-faced forgery being carried on so openly in a village backyard is surprising.

Other brooch types include the huge silver shoulder brooches

48   *Relief of Aha, daughter of Halafta, son of Bar'a, A.D. 161. Palmyra*

which were a striking feature of the dress of Norican women(*46e*), and bronze brooches such as a first century type with the maker's name on the bow above the hinge(*46g*). The so-called knee-brooches(*46h*), favourites along the Rhine-Danube frontier in the second and third centuries, and the later crossbow brooches, were widespread. In Britain and the Rhineland attractive jewellery was made from jet, probably Whitby jet, manufactured at York into pendants, beads, pins, rings and armlets, was exported to Germany as finished products. The hairpins would look particularly effective. Pendants of small bears or other animals or carvings in relief with busts of one or two people are not uncommon, some of them perhaps gifts to mark weddings or anniversaries(*46f*). Bracelets studded with pearls found in Spain were made from Spanish jet.

Metalwork

A smith or two must have been at work in all but the very smallest settlements. Silver and the best bronze vessels were made in quantity at Italian centres such as Capua, and later in Gaul at Lyons or in Germany at Gressenich near Aachen, and traded over a wide area both inside and outside the Roman frontiers. The more ordinary pots, kettles and tools, however, were made by local craftsmen to suit their customers' preferences. For these scrap-metal was often collected, melted down and used again. Inscriptions record bronze smelters at Nîmes and Narbonne.

Bronze foundries in Noricum have been identified at Solva and Ovilava while discoveries along the Danube in Pannonia give some idea of provincial bronze-working. In the colony at Aquincum a furnace was found in the market place with scrap metal and finished articles. Moulds and castings have been discovered at Brigetio and the keys and ornamental mountings for carriages made here are found all over the province. Some craftsmen seem to have started by repairing imported vessels and graduated on to making new ones. At Carnuntum small items such as medical instruments, pins and brooches were produced in large numbers. One of the Sens reliefs depicts a bronze worker's shop with large dishes and a tripod; here a customer is buying a small jar.

The blacksmith is a favourite subject for sculptors. One from Noricum, Nammonius Mussa, appears on his tombstone found at Karlsdorf near Graz, clasping hammer and pincers and accom-

49   Bellicus the smith. Sens

panied by his wife Calandina. Other tombstones from Autun and Nuits-St-Georges also have the tools of their trade. Another smith from York is at work at his anvil; he may be a military smith or even a representation of the traditionally lame god Vulcan. But Bellicus son of Bellator from Sens was certainly mortal although possibly also lame(*49*): nearly bald, except where some hair falls on to his right shoulder, he appears to be wearing only one boot, the other foot perhaps being covered with a sock; behind his right leg a pet dog seeks cover from the menacing paw of a cat. Hoards of iron tools as well as the numerous implements found on town and country sites provide practical illustration of the blacksmith's skill.

MINERAL RESOURCES

Where did the raw material for all this metal working come from? In Britain, copper, tin, lead and a little gold were found. Spain was the richest province of all, famous for its gold, silver, lead, tin and copper mines. More iron, copper and lead occur in north-east France and the mountains near the Rhine, and lead and zinc deposits near Aachen led to the manufacture of brass at Gressenich from about A.D. 75. Iron of a natural steel-like quality is known from Noricum and at the native site on the Magdalensberg, near the later Roman city founded in A.D. 45 at the foot of the hill at Virunum (near Klagenfurt), a busy trading centre grew up around Norican iron and metal work. In the first century B.C. traders came to it from far afield.

On the walls of the houses in the business quarter graffiti record a remarkable series of transactions. For example, 355 iron axes each weighing 1 kilo were credited to Ombrio. Sineros of Aquileia bought 110 cups and Orosius from Volubilis 110 dishes. Iron anvils, jugs, copper plates and hooks are also listed. Loans recorded include money lent to the son of Sextus from Lanuvium on 31 January repayable by 1 July, and a sum lent to someone else in July was due on 15 October. A few graffiti are concerned with other matters. Proculus asks for an oracle, and in one building L. Opaius Verrucosus made a holy niche for Mercury with his own hands.

Silver and iron mines seem to have been worked in Pannonia, and in Transylvania the gold mines were important. Macedonia was renowned in antiquity for its gold and silver but by the Roman period the mines seem to have been largely worked out. The same applies to many of the deposits in Asia Minor. North Africa possesses few mineral resources but gold was found in Egypt and also imported from Nubia, and lead and silver were mined near the Red Sea.

MINING

Some information is available about Roman mining methods and working conditions. Normally these vitally important metals belonged to the state and their exploitation was carried out by the emperor's procurators who adapted general imperial policies to local conditions; alternatively contractors might lease a mine and work it themselves or lease small holdings to individuals. In such cases a 50 per cent share of the product had to be paid to the state. The type of development varied from province to province.

In Britain production in the lead mines started under army control soon after the conquest. The reason for this was the quest for silver, usually obtained from smelting lead ore. At first the invaders must have been sadly disappointed as the proportion of silver in British lead is so small it is hardly worth extracting. Lead, however was a valuable mineral in its own right necessary for water pipes and linings for baths and cisterns, and also used for roofs, coffins, caskets and pewter vessels. It became an important export, the pigs or ingots stamped with military stamps or contractors' names known to be British, being found in France at St Valéry-sur-Somme and Chalons-sur-Saône, and probably at Lillebonne and Toulouse. Gaul produced only a small amount of lead and so would have been an important market for supplies from Spain and Britain. British supplies may have been shipped up the rivers Seine and Saône, and further south a land route may have been followed from Toulouse across to Narbonne. From there the lead may have travelled on to Italy; a cistern at Pompeii is probably made from British lead.

By the end of the first century A.D. the Spanish gold mines were producing 9,400 kilos (2,900 lb) annually, and systems of aqueducts used to loosen and wash down the gold-bearing rock have been identified. For silver, lead and copper, deep mines were dug. Drainage was provided by wooden wheels with containers attached to the rim, turned by hand. At Rio Tinto a system with eight wheels was found, working in pairs at different levels. A relief discovered at the mining centre of Linares (Castulo) where a complex system of workings exists, depicts a foreman and his gang of eight walking down a gallery two abreast (50); one man carries a lamp, another a pick; the tall foreman has large pincers, a bell and possibly a lantern. Gold and silver were needed for the coinage, and Spanish lead also travelled far afield to Italy, Germany and North Africa.

50 Spanish miners. Linares

The Spanish copper-mines have left us some of the best evidence for Roman mining processes. Many of these were in the southern province of Baetica, the most Romanized area. The best ore came from round the capital, Cordoba, and this was used for the coinage. A shaft over 213 m (688 ft) deep was sunk to find it. Further west at Sotiel Coronada are some rectangular shafts cut in soft rock in stages, each stage of under a metre possibly indicating a day's work. The miners seem to have been lowered into them with a windlass. The low galleries were up to a metre wide with lamp-niches near the roof. Galleries might be cut to link up with several shafts and in making these, errors sometimes occurred in the surveying, causing awkward corners.

At Tharsis, west of Sotiel Coronada, small prospecting shafts were found with hand and toe holds showing that they were climbed without a ladder. The debris and ore were carried in esparto grass baskets on the miners' backs. Walls and roofs were supported by pit-props of local oak. Sulphur dioxide gas at these levels was a danger and special ventilation shafts were necessary. When accidents occurred rescue was difficult, and in one mine skeletons of 18 miners were found, killed by a rock fall. Fifty miners died in a similar disaster in the cinnabar mines at Sizma in Galatia.

Tin, one of the rarer metals, essential for making bronze, was an important product of north-west Spain and northern Portugal. Mining of all kinds flourished in Spain from Augustus onwards, and in Flavian times diminishing supplies from Greece and Asia Minor led to further development. When conditions of trade reduced supplies during the disruptions of the third century, increased output of tin and lead from Britain and Sardinia helped to fill the gap.

Mine management
By the time of the Flavians, the imperial government had drawn up regulations controlling conditions in the mines. As well as slaves and criminals there is evidence of free labour, with Spaniards signing on at Rio Tinto for six-month periods.

Further west from Tharsis, at Aljustrel in Portugal, was the pyrites mine at Vipasca worked for copper or silver, and here two early second-century bronze inscriptions relating to its working were found. Apparently the mine was worked by lessees who had to make a down payment of the state's half share before they began to smelt any ore. For silver diggings this sum was 4,000 sesterces. Work must be continuous, and holdings left unworked reverted to the state. A lessee might take partners on condition that each paid his fair share and measures were prescribed to ensure this. Ore could only be mined in daylight and must be moved to the furnaces in daytime. A slave stealing ore would be whipped or sold; a free man had his property confiscated; either were forbidden to go near a mine again. Similar penalties applied to anyone making the mines unsafe. Pit-props, timbering and drainage channels had to be kept in good condition.

The other inscription relates to amenities: the procurators licensed barbers, cobblers, and fullers. The concessionaires who ran the baths had to open them for women in the morning at the fee of one *as*, and the rest of the day for men at half-price. The procurator's employees were admitted free. A plentiful supply of hot water had to be provided and buildings and equipment kept clean and in good order, subject to fair wear and tear. If repairs prevented the baths being used the lessee had his rent reduced. The mention of women reminds us of the miners' wives and families, and the inscription notes that the schoolmasters at Vipasca were to be exempt from taxation. A last item relates to those exploiting slag-dumps and small deposits, perhaps trying to bring back into operation abandoned mines or find new ones.

THE SUPPLY OF LABOUR

Sometimes workers were difficult to find.so in the early second century some of the Pirustae, a large tribe living in mining areas in southern Bosnia and northern Montenegro, were moved to western Dacia to work important gold mines there. At Veres-patak a series of mid second-century inscribed waxed tablets have survived, and one of these identifies the town as the Roman Alburnus Major and also as' the settlement of the conscripted Pirustae. Other tablets are concerned with the purchase of a girl by a legionary from Apulum, and the sale of half a house, and various loans. Perhaps the most interesting is the contract between a free labourer called Memmius and the lessee of a mine-shaft, Aurelius Adjutor. Memmius was illiterate so Flavius Secundinus, perhaps a clerk at the mine office, wrote it out for him. He undertook to work well from 20 May to 15 November A.D. 164 for 70 denarii and board, payable in instalments. If he quit or took days off he would be fined five sesterces for each day, and if

Adjutor did not pay him, he too would be fined for the delay, subject to three days' grace. The wax tablets may have been hidden during the Marcomannic invasions in which some of the miners may have been carried off. The mines at Verespatak were abandoned. In one of them was an underground room with rock-cut benches where the miners lived. Lying on one was a skeleton.

In Memmius it seems we have an example of a free man finding a job, and this must sometimes have been a problem for those who were not slaves directed by masters nor freedmen aided by patrons. It is clear that craftsmen working with unusual techniques or in expensive materials suffered a serious risk of under-employment, and this must be one reason why mosaicists, masons, sculptors etc., tended to travel. Potters and glass makers also moved around and used their skills to start up new factories in the provinces. When business expanded or the craftsman grew old such skills had to be handed on, preferably to a son or a young friend or relative who had been adopted as heir. Otherwise slaves had to be bought or young apprentices accepted for training. Sometimes a premium was paid but usually the learner could be usefully employed doing simple jobs to earn his keep. A formal agreement was made between the master-craftsman and the apprentice's parents, guardian, or master, as in some cases slaves were trained in this way to make more money for their owners later on. This agreement had to be officially registered. In some cases a tax was payable on apprentices.

Our knowledge of apprenticeship agreements and conditions of work is substantially based on information from Egyptian papyri so that it may be biased and only apply to certain trades. Training varied in length: two or three years for a weaver, up to ten for a skilled sculptor or smith. Unlike ordinary contracts for hired labour, a fixed number of days off for public holidays were allowed, varying between 18 and 27. Unauthorized absences were punished by fines, and the time might have to be made up. It is not clear what happened in the case of illness. The master-craftsman was bound to provide instruction, and to present his pupil before a panel of three craftsmen for approval at the end of training. Then the pupil might work on as a hired man, gaining experience until the opportunity arose to set up on his own. In the emergencies of the later years of the Empire many occupations became legally hereditary; skilled workers had to stay with their communities and no longer sought work elsewhere.

GUILDS

Inscriptions sometimes mention members of *collegia* or guilds of workmen, so it should be emphasized that these were not guilds in the medieval sense. The Roman authorities were very nervous of any gatherings which might have political purposes and spread sedition, so these were strictly forbidden. Even public meetings before elections had to be presided over by a magistrate. A law attributed to Julius Caesar laid down that *collegia* must be licensed, originally by the Senate in Rome, later by the emperor and his representatives. The Roman guilds were primarily religious, and were probably only allowed to meet once a month to worship a patron deity. They combined these occasions, however, with a strong social life, contributing to the occasional dinner, building up plenty of hierarchy and precedence among the members and gaining a definite status in town life. Many of them were burial clubs, their members making regular payments to ensure themselves an adequate funeral, often in a tomb or part of a cemetery belonging to their association. The organization of the burial club at Lanuvium in 136 is well known because its bye-laws have survived. Less familiar, perhaps, is a notice posted up in Alburnus Major in 167: it seems that only 17 remained of a burial club founded by 54 members. These survivors had ceased to attend meetings or make contributions, so the officers gave notice that they were dissolving the society, having divided the last of the funds among the members who were reminded that no money and no coffins remained, and requests for burial could no longer be accepted.

Collegia were usually made up of members of the same craft or trade living in the same town, but they had nothing to do with apprenticeship, keeping up standards of craftsmanship or making representations for better wages and conditions. A slave could be included with his master's permission and the burial clubs were largely made up of slaves and freedmen. Like many cities, guilds had patrons, influential people often of a higher social status than the members and not concerned with their day-to-day activities. Patrons might receive the title of 'father of the guild' and it was hoped that they would prove generous. When these hopes were realized, the *collegium* would show its appreciation in the usual way by putting up a statue to its benefactor. The *fabri* (craftsmen) at Narbonne did this in A.D. 149 for Sextus Fadius Secundus Musa, a distinguished citizen who had held all the local honours. Apparently it gave him great pleasure for below the inscription on the base appears a copy of a letter he wrote to them on 1 October sending them a gift of 16,000 sesterces to be invested at $12\frac{1}{2}\%$, the interest to be used for an annual banquet of the guild on his birthday, 27 April. On this date in 150, accompanied by his son and grandson, he brought the gift and the first year's interest and deposited it in their treasury. In return a copy of his letter had to be inscribed on his statue base and on a bronze tablet put up in a temple. The letter ends with good wishes to all.

The patron's gifts were often the chief source of revenue for a *collegium* treasury, backed up by contributions made by officials on taking office. The members' entrance fees amounted to little, perhaps only consisting of an amphora of wine of varying quality. A small monthly contribution was also expected but there was sometimes trouble in collecting this. Sometimes small fines were imposed on members who disobeyed the president or on officials who forgot to call meetings.

One purpose for any funds not tied down for other uses was to construct the guild's own temple or hall (*schola*) where it could have meetings and put up the statues of benefactors. A city would often donate land to a useful guild, and until they could afford to build, the members could meet under the porticos of the basilica or the forum. Evidence for several probable *scholae* has been found at Aquincum. The one belonging to the *centonarii* (cloth-workers) was on the first floor of a building inside the south gate. When fire destroyed it in the second half of the third century the hall and its furnishings fell into the cellar. Among them were the bronze parts of the pneumatic organ (see p. 90) with an inscribed bronze tablet relating that it was given to the guild in 228 by the president Caius Julius Viatorinus, a former *aedile* of Aquincum.

For a glimpse of the menu at one of the banquets which took place in the *scholae* we can turn to a Dacian wax tablet found at Verespatak. This is a bill detailing an outlay of 169 denarii: 5 lambs cost 18 denarii, a sucking pig 5, 2 or 3 denarii for white bread, 97 denarii for *vin ordinaire* and 2 for better wine, 1 for salad, $\frac{1}{2}$ each for salt and vinegar, 2 or 3 for incense – the rest is lost. This banquet would have been a small-scale affair for the gold-miners. Rich corporations included distributions of money (*sportulae*) to their diners.

A survey of the lists of *collegia* known from inscriptions gives a still more detailed picture of the occupations of the peoples of the Empire. The most important guilds were those of the *fabri* and *centonarii*. The *fabri* included a wide range of craftsmen, particularly those working on building sites. The *centonarii* originally seem to have made patchwork garments from old clothes, but their activities may have been extended to include those concerned with the various branches of the textile trade. In many towns the two *collegia* acted as the fire-brigade aided by the *dendrophori*, lumbermen or timber merchants. All three are known in Dacia at Apulum, in Pannonia at Emona, and in Gaul at Nîmes and Vienne.

Also connected with a flourishing textile industry were a variety of guilds recorded in Asia Minor. Wool-washers, workers, dealers, fullers and dyers are all known from places like Hierapolis, and linen-workers from Tarsus, towel-weavers from Ephesus, and workers in hemp from Cyzicus. Related to the *dendrophori* were the *fabri tignarii*, or wood-workers. Three of their *collegia* are recorded from upper Germany, timber from the Black Forest no doubt supplying the ones at Baden-Baden. Elsewhere we hear of cabinet-makers.

In Asia Minor were nailsmiths at Hierapolis, metal-bed-makers at Tralles, and makers of coral images at Magnesia-under-Sipylus. Guilds of gardeners are also known. Other less commonly attested *collegia* include the litter-bearers at Sarmize-getusa and the *collegium fociorum* of Cologne, variously interpreted as stokers of the public baths, makers of kitchen utensils or cooks. The great guilds of the *nautae* and *navicularii* who organized water transport by river and sea, and the *collegia* of businessmen will be discussed later (pp. 167, 169).

STRIKES

A small amount of evidence of labour disputes survives. At the end of the second century the people of Ephesus were plunged into disorder by a bakers' strike. In an edict the governor reproved the evil-speaking in the market place of seditious groups of bakers who deserved punishment; but as the chief consideration was the bread-supply, if they went back to work they would not be punished. However, anyone in future found attending illegal meetings or causing a riot would pay the penalty.

An edict from Pergamum complains of delays in completing contract work on buildings, possibly due to strikes: an enquiry was held and those who attended it were leniently treated, while others were fined; apparently the workers had individual contracts with the various employers including the town architect. Another second-century example from Miletus had a different solution. It seems that a group of workers led by their foreman were erecting the vaults and arches over the columns in the theatre, superintended by the public overseer and architect. On account of a grievance or perhaps of an offer of higher paid work elsewhere, they considered ceasing work but before reaching a decision they agreed to consult the famous oracle of Apollo at Didyma. The oracle advised sacrifices to Athene and Heracles and the seeking of further expert advice. Unfortunately the outcome is not known, perhaps the religious observances provided a cooling-off period in which the grievance was settled or the wages increased.

6

Country life

In contrast to urban life, which in many parts of the Empire was a Roman innovation, country-dwellers were aware of far fewer drastic changes in their mode of existence arising from Roman rule. The evidence for these is less impressive as, apart from the writers specifically dealing with agriculture, the surviving literary sources are largely the work of city authors who tended either to neglect the subject or poke fun at the rustics. Official documents, inscriptions and reliefs help to fill some of the gaps but, as with the poorer townsfolk, it is difficult to recapture many details about the peasant population. Yet agriculture was the Empire's major industry upon which all else depended, and the purchase of land was considered to be the safest and the one really reputable form of investment.

Naturally the size of the farm unit varied very much. In Italy some smallholdings worked by one farmer and his family existed throughout the Roman period, and this seems also to have been the case in much of the Empire with farmers dwelling in isolation or gathered together into villages. On the less productive land or in the remoter areas such settlements continued, but on richer soils many of them were eventually swallowed up by large landowners. Some of the inhabitants then left the land or became tenants and lost their independence. Medium sized farms producing several different crops with domestic animals and sometimes vine and olive plantations had a better chance of survival. Records exist from the first century B.C. onwards of estates, some of very large size, belonging to private owners and later often of imperial property. The part played by the cultivated areas immediately outside towns and forts must also be remembered as a source of food supplies.

In many parts of the Empire agricultural methods were little affected by Roman rule, although some new crops were introduced and larger farming units developed. The chief benefits which affected the provinces as a whole were more general. The end of tribal warfare and the development of urbanization encouraged the growth of permanent settlement and an increase in the population. Better communications enabled the farmers to take advantage of new and bigger local markets to meet the demands of townsfolk and the army. Drainage or irrigation and cheaper and more plentiful tools also improved production. The area which has been most studied from an agricultural point of view is Italy, and as usual, it is difficult to know how far Italian ideas applied in the provinces. One can only guess at the extent to which the farming manuals of Cato, Varro, Columella and Palladius, based on centuries of practical experience, circulated among educated provincial landowners. Otherwise our knowledge of provincial farming operations largely depends on the illustrations provided by reliefs and the great series of African mosaics.

The Roman authors mentioned above lay stress on the need to study the soil and choose the most suitable crops for each type. Barley for example, needed dry, loose soil, while heavier, damper conditions were needed for wheat. The ground was fed with animal manures, and might also be improved by dressings of marl (a natural mixture of clay and carbonate of lime). Columella mentions an uncle who developed vineyards near Cordoba in Spain by using marl on gravelly soil, and gravel on dense chalky land. Pasture was a problem in many provinces, necessitating a constant search for fodder with migrations of flocks and herds from winter to summer grazing. With insufficient pasture the animal manure available was limited. Even when eked out by compost and green crops such as lupine or lucerne there was not enough. Hence we find experiments in crop-rotation being carried out side by side with the older methods of allowing some land to lie fallow.

FARM IMPLEMENTS

Whichever methods were used to obtain fertility constant cultivation was needed. Fresh ground might be first broken with picks, mattocks or the heavy two-pronged drag-hoe(*51b*) and then dug or ploughed. Long handled spades appear on some

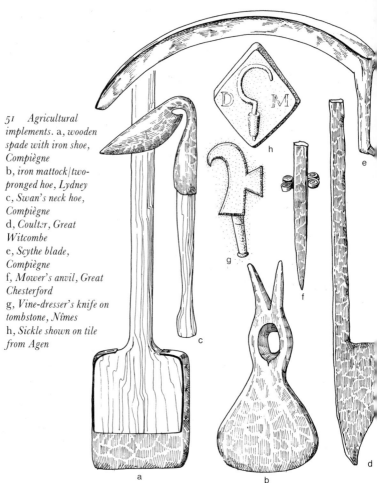

51   *Agricultural implements.* a, *wooden spade with iron shoe, Compiègne* b, *iron mattock/two-pronged hoe, Lydney* c, *Swan's neck hoe, Compiègne* d, *Coulter, Great Witcombe* e, *Scythe blade, Compiègne* f, *Mower's anvil, Great Chesterford* g, *Vine-dresser's knife on tombstone, Nîmes* h, *Sickle shown on tile from Agen*

reliefs, notably one from Arlon. Actual discoveries from Verulamium in Britain and Compiègne in France have proved that the blades might either be entirely of iron, or, for reasons of economy, a wooden blade was given an iron sheath(*51a*).

Several types of plough are mentioned by Latin authors, but the descriptions are far from explicit. One variety which loosened and broke up the soil was particularly suitable for lighter soils or hilly country. It was made of wood and the iron plough-shares used with it are often found. Usually it was drawn by a pair of yoked oxen and a North African mosaic shows a plough of this type in use(*52*). At the top a man is breaking up clods of earth

52   Mosaic showing ploughing, Cherchel

while on the right the ploughman is at work. Below a man is broadcasting seed on the right, with the plough following him and ploughing it in. A mosaic from Oudna, Tunisia, shows the ploughman and his team returning home with other farm animals(*53*). A spare plough with the yoke attached at the top is leaning against the building. Other ploughing scenes appear in relief at Mactar (Tunisia), and Seica-Mica (Hungary).

For heavier soil a more elaborate type of plough was developed with a knife-shaped piece of iron called the coulter added to cut through the ground in front of the share(*51d*). The coulter seems to have been a Roman invention and judging from the number found it was extensively used on the clays of Roman Britain, Gaul and Germany. Pliny mentions a wheeled plough used in Raetia as another innovation.

Several ploughings were needed to produce a suitable tilth for sowing. Seed was sown by hand and the sower on the Cherchel mosaic(*52*) is scattering it with both hands from a basket hung round his neck. The main cereal sowings were made in autumn, with spring sowing in the cooler provinces or if the crop failed. Hoeing to break up and loosen the soil, keep down weeds, and conserve moisture was very necessary.

53   Mosaic with scenes of agricultural life. Oudna

Harvesting

For harvesting cereals the farmer used the balanced sickle, a
Roman invention in which the weight of the curved blade is
carefully balanced with the handle. It appears in relief on a
Roman brick from a funeral monument at Agen(*51h*) and on a
tomb relief from Ghirza. Varro describes how the grain might be
cut near the root, then the ears cut off and the straw left to dry,
perhaps for use in thatching. Another method cut the stalks in the
centre, leaving stubble for grazing and keeping straw for litter.

Grain cut with straw attached had to be threshed on circular
threshing floors, the best of which were flagged. These have been
found on villa sites in Britain and elsewhere. Fig. *54* shows the
operation at Zliten in Tripolitania: the foreman is chivying on
the herdsman and two unwilling oxen, while the lady of the
manor urges on the workers trying to control a pair of horses
trampling out the grain. The alternative method of threshing
with the *tribulum*, a heavy wooden sledge studded underneath
with flints or nails, may have been easier. For cutting the hay-
harvest Pliny mentions two varieties of scythe, a small Italian
one-handed variety which could also cut brambles, and a larger
one found on estates in Gaul. Blades belonging to the second type
and varying in size have been found in Britain and Germany.

54 Mosaic showing threshing. Zliten

THE GRAIN SUPPLY

Wheat and barley were the most important cereals grown in the Roman Empire. Cato, Varro and other writers stress the need to keep the best of the harvest for seed, and quality and yield seem to have gradually improved as a result of experiments with imported grain. For making bread, wheat was preferred as it produces finer, whiter flour. Emmer and spelt were also used but these are hulled wheats so the hulls (glumes) had to be removed, usually by roasting. Emmer, one of the most ancient wheats, cultivated since Neolithic times, was widespread in Europe, round the Mediterranean and in the Near East. Spelt came into Italy from northern Europe, and oats, a hardier form of emmer, were cultivated in the north-western provinces. Spelt is also mentioned in Asia Minor. Roman expansion helped to widen the distribution of such crops; oats, for example, were probably introduced into Scotland by the Roman army.

To keep the citizens of Rome fed considerable supplies of grain had to be imported, and rumours of any interruption of this traffic through war, bad weather, or poor harvests were liable to cause riots and even shake the imperial throne. Some cities also followed Rome's example in making public provision for essential foodstuffs. In the early Empire much of the grain was collected as a tax, the *annona*. The grain was usually transported by sea so many favours were granted to the big shipping firms involved in such traffic. Pliny lists the areas supplying grain as Boeotia, Sicily, Africa, Gaul, Thrace, Syria and Egypt.

Barley was also important, particularly for animal food and beer-making. In the Mediterranean area it was more extensively grown than wheat until the demands of the cities led to increased wheat production. In the colder north rye was developed from barley and spread in a small way into Italy late in the Empire; the Mediterranean climate, however, does not suit it. Groats made from emmer were a favourite food and millet was also eaten. This was a spring-sown crop which could be planted in an emergency if the winter wheat crop failed. A little rice was grown near the Syrian coast but without extensive artificial irrigation its possibilities were limited.

The storage of grain received serious consideration. In the damper areas it had to be dried, and drying floors heated hypocaust fashion are found not infrequently in Britain. Granaries should be dry, well-ventilated, free from vermin, and secure from theft. The army soon realized the need to safeguard food supplies and long, narrow buildings, their raised floors resting on wooden piles or stone supports, are a feature of many forts and fortresses. The grain was probably stored in bins arranged on either side of a central gangway.

Outside Italy much less is known of civilian granaries. One with six rooms at Djemila in Algeria was founded in A.D. 199, according to an inscription, but this may have been a store for a Roman official rather than for the town's own supplies. At Trier a fourth-century store beside the river housed the grain supply for the surrounding area. On other sites grain may have been kept in lofts above buildings used for other puposes.

SHEEP AND OTHER LIVESTOCK

The importance of wool for the textile trade has already been discussed and sheep were also important as a source of milk, cheese and manure. Several breeds are mentioned and distinctions are made between hairy and woolly coated sheep and different colours. Columella's uncle seems to have experimented with a cross between wild African rams and fat-tailed Tarentine sheep kept on his estate near Cadiz. Wool produced locally for the Laodicean textile industry is described as raven-black.

Columella and the other authorities advise the farmer on sheep management in some detail, discriminating between large numbers scattered over the grazing lands and flocks kept near towns. Lambs born in the large herds numbering up to a thousand might be added to the flock, while nearer towns milk and cheese were more important and would be sent with young lambs to market. One of the scenes of the Oudna mosaic (53) shows a shepherd milking while another plays a pipe. Another shepherd is mentioned in an inscription from Tugia in Spain: he carried heavy responsibilities as he had to organize supplies to feed his workers and women to cook for them; he must have been literate as he would need to keep accounts, and possessed veterinary skill to advise his assistants, especially at lambing time. At Mainz the landowner Marcus Terentius put up a tombstone for his freedman and shepherd, Jucundus, which depicts him with his dog leading his flock to pasture through a forest (55). This inscription relates how at the age of 30 Jucundus was murdered by a slave who then drowned himself in the Main.

55   Shepherd with sheep. Mainz

For milk and cheese goats were even more important than sheep as their yield is greater. Because they are more delicate animals, the herds were smaller to avoid the spread of disease. Both kids and lambs might be hand-reared. It is difficult to discriminate between the two when assemblages of animal bones from Roman sites are examined, but there was certainly a steady demand for kid-meat. Hair from the long-haired goats of Phrygia and Cilicia was used for ropes, sacking, and horse-blankets.

Pork was the Roman's favourite meat and there are many different recipes for all the eatable portions of the pig. Sucking-pigs were much esteemed and some of the hams imported into Italy from Gaul and Spain have already been noted (p. 102). Goats and pigs in small numbers could be kept by the poorer members of the community. Herds of swine of up to 150 are mentioned by Varro, and Columella supplies much good advice. The need for each sow and her piglets to have separate sties was realized, with walls high enough to stop the pigs climbing out.

The most important working animal was the ox. Columella describes how it should be broken in and trained to walk at the steady pace needed for pulling the plough or a wagon. Next it had to be accustomed to the yoke and then set to work with a more experienced animal. An obstinate ox might be yoked between two older beasts until it had learned to obey orders. (Oxen tend to prefer one side of the yoke to the other, and problems still arise for farmers in primitive communities today when a right-hand or a left-hand ox dies and another suitable animal is not available.) The oxen were left on the farm as there was work for them during most of the year, especially during the spring and autumn ploughings.

Cows might also pull the plough. Their milk was not as highly esteemed for drinking or cheese-making as that of sheep or goats. In Italy beef was not popular, but more was eaten in the north-western provinces. Hides were needed for many purposes and lard also figured in Roman diets. Some mention of different breeds is made by ancient authors but these are difficult to identify. The Epirote cattle from Greece were highly esteemed and imported into Italy. The small pre-Roman ox found in many areas occurs in collections of animal bones from the provinces, but remains of larger animals are also found and may represent breeds brought in to improve the stock. From Spain a letter from Hadrian to the town council of Tarragona prescribes the punishment to be meted out to cattle-thieves. Ox, pig and sheep were also important as sacrificial animals.

Of the farm animals not kept for food the most useful was the donkey who could be used to turn the mill, carry manure to the fields and bring in the crops. On lighter soils in Africa or Spain he could also pull the plough. As a pack-animal he could take produce to market, and trains of donkeys were also used to transport pottery, wine etc. long distances. Horses were not usually employed for farm work. For transport purposes the mule, the result of a cross between a mare and a jack-donkey, was a far better investment than the horse, less nervous, more easily trained, and with greater stamina.

POULTRY

Poultry keeping was an important activity and Columella discusses it thoroughly. The best breeds were obtained by crossing Greek cocks with Italian hens. The Greek birds were also the finest for cock-fighting. A flock of 200 is recommended, looked after by one poultry-keeper with an old woman or a youth to help him. The importance of hygiene was realized, and that each bird should have its own perch and nest in well-ventilated hen-houses with enclosed yards; also that a careful record should be kept of egg-production and when eggs were put under a broody hen. There was a good market for both eggs and chickens. They appear on Gaulish reliefs either on the dining-table as the

56 Mosaic showing house. Tabarka

chicken at Arlon (*frontis.*) or being brought as payment in kind by tenants. Ducks and geese were also kept wherever conditions permitted, and goose down was much prized. Less frequent in the drier climate of Africa, ducks are shown beside a stream on one of the mosaics from Tabarka (*56*). The African hen mentioned by Varro is probably a guinea-fowl and his author also notes the raising in aviaries of a variety of table-birds for the gourmet, varying in size from field-fares or quails to swans and peacocks. Pigeons were reared in separate pigeon-houses. Birds were also kept for pleasure, blackbirds or nightingales for their songs and doves and peafowl for their appearance.

FODDER

The provision of adequate fodder for the farm animals was a perpetual problem, especially in Italy and round the Mediterranean. Broad beans and other varieties of bean, chick-peas and turnips were grown for both human and animal food. From the writings of Cato and Columella it has been possible to work out the rations of the vital working oxen through the year. The food ranges from chaff and grapeskins eked out with hay in December when the team was not working, to the same with fresh leaves for the next four months, with a good increase of hay once the ploughing started and fresh green forage when obtainable. This should be pulled by hand so the plants would continue to grow. Elm, ash and poplar leaves were best, oak and laurel a last resort. The picture is one of considerable anxiety in case supplies did not hold out.

Sheep and cows were pastured as far as possible in sheltered areas in winter, otherwise they too had to share the leaves. Swine roamed the forests eating beech mast and acorns, and were fattened on beans, or turned out into an orchard to eat apples, pears or figs. It seems that the livestock was brought through the winter successfully. Britain has provided evidence that the practice of autumn-killing, in which all but the minimum stock needed to carry on the herd were slaughtered, was not necessary.

MARKET GARDENING

Other agricultural pursuits included the cultivation of the vegetable garden and orchard. Both were enclosed by a hedge or wall where possible to keep out thieves and animals. Mosaics, literature and material excavated out of rubbish pits provide a good list of the results of these activities. In addition to those already mentioned, lettuce, cabbages, carrots, radishes, asparagus and many herbs were known, and figs, apples, pears, apricots, peaches, plums, quinces, mulberries, cherries, almonds and nut trees. Plants were grown from seeds and cuttings, and fruit trees were much improved by grafting varieties sometimes brought from afar. Fig. 56 shows fruit trees growing near a villa.

OLIVES

In many provinces two more specialised crops were of major importance, the olive and the grape. Olives grow well in any soil apart from heavy clay, so long as there is good drainage and the climate is right. Hill slopes can be used, and where the soil was suitable, grain or other crops were often planted between the rows of trees. Cato and Pliny mention a number of different varieties of olive suited to different areas. Fruit could be picked when the trees were seven years old. It bruises easily so it had to be carefully picked, and one of the Oudna mosaics shows a negro pulling down branches with a rope and knocking the olives off with a pair of long canes. The Seasons mosaic found near Sousse(60) shows Winter in a frame of olive sprays, and on her left a man is either picking up olives or windfalls or planting beans.

Once established the trees needed so little attention that the small farmers could profit from the crops without losing much time from other activities. The gathered olives were cleaned and taken in baskets to the oil factory, lightly pressed to extract as many stones as possible, and then put though the oil-mill. The

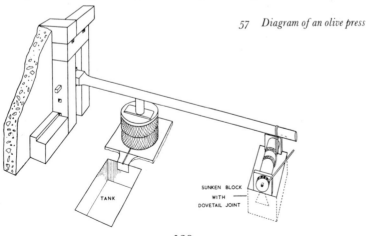

57   Diagram of an olive press

TANK

SUNKEN BLOCK
WITH ———
DOVETAIL JOINT

resulting pulp was put into rush-lined baskets and placed under the press(57). This stood on a stone floor with channels of varying length along which the oil flowed into a cistern. After clarifying it was drained into a second cistern and then decanted into storage jars.

Roman Africa produced oil in abundance. The Carthaginians had also cultivated the olive, but under the early Empire the chief emphasis was on grain production. Juvenal comments disparagingly on the quality of African oil at this period. With the use of better equipment the quality was much improved and the oil export trade reached its peak in the second and third centuries. Many traces of oil presses have been found in both town and country, more than 50 in Volubilis alone (see p. 69). The most important areas for olive oil production lay further east. In eastern Algeria near Thagura and Madauros a number of presses have been found in a comparatively small area; in one house at Madauros, as well as the mill and the supports for two presses, a stable was found with mangers for seven animals and also a wagon shed. More presses have been found on imperial domains in northern Tunisia, where the Roman frontier was pushed further out into the desert in the south to give more room for olive groves. In Tripolitania, where the climate was too dry for much grain production, olives were the main crop.

In the drier areas of Africa efforts were made to conserve water. Aerial photographs of the area south-west of the Aures mountains in Algeria show a maze of irrigation channels into which flood waters from the melting mountain snows were directed. Elsewhere, when rain did come it flooded water-courses which were normally dry. These water-courses were sometimes dammed. Wells were sunk to tap water at deep levels, and rainfall was caught and directed into deep cisterns.

VINES

The grape had a wider distribution than the olive, and different varieties were available for the Romans to experiment with until the most suitable were found for the different provinces, from the cool climate and early frost of the Moselle to the hot dry areas of Spain and North Africa. Pliny gives many examples of vines suitable for different climates, advising the farmer to allow for the individual peculiarities of each. To yield well the soil round the base of the vine must be kept well cultivated and this operation is

58 Mosaic of vineyard. Cherchel

depicted on one of the Cherchel mosaics(*58*). The plants had to be supported in various ways, sometimes round a circle of canes as on the lower part of the same mosaic(*58*) or on the scenes from Tabarka.

When ripe, the grapes had to be gathered as speedily as possible and extra workers must have been employed. The fruit was first put in a vat for crushing, and treading the grapes is a favourite subject for artists. Three cupids appear doing just this among the decoration on the Weiden sarcophagus(*99* and p. *214*). The residue was strained and put in baskets under the wine-press, a contraption similar to that used for olive pressing. From the press the wine was channelled into large pottery jars and kept for 90 days for the first fermentation. Then it might be stored in barrels for anything up to five years. Measured into amphorae it would then be sold. In some cases it was transported in an ox-skin mounted on a frame on a wagon.

THE WINE TRADE

Travelling round the Empire we find wine-production important in Greece, Palestine, Babylonia and Syria. Viticulture was already flourishing in Spain during the first century B.C. Vines were brought from Africa and Italy; an inscription mentions a procurator entrusted with the task of superintending the planting of cuttings from the vines from which the famous Italian Falernian was made. The Mediterranean coast, south-west

Spain and Portugal were the chief wine-growing areas exporting their products to Italy. At home Spaniards, Gauls, Britons and Germans also drank beer (*cervesia*), and *cervesarii*, brewers, are known from inscriptions at Metz and Trier. Mead, made from honey, and cider were also drunk.

Some indifferent wine was produced near the Greek colony at Marseilles as early as the sixth century B.C. Diodorus tells us that when wine was imported by Italian traders into early first-century Gaul it was rapturously received. The people drank it neat instead of diluted with water as in Italy, and they drank it in large quantities, buying it by the boat or wagon load, and paying for it with slaves. By the first century B.C. the vine itself was being cultivated in Gaul in two main areas. The oldest French vineyards are believed to be beside the river Tarn near Albi, especially at Gaillac where local potters were making amphorae during the early years of Augustus's reign, perhaps for the sparkling white wine still produced there; it may have travelled down the river into the Garonne and so reached Bordeaux. The other area is in the territory of the Allobroges by the Rhône between Valence and Vienne, and this produced a red wine noted by Celsus in the first century A.D.

By the second half of the first century A.D. Pliny remarks that a veritable chemist's shop of herbs and other noxious ingredients was mixed with wine from Beziers, near Narbonne, perhaps an early form of the apéritif, and a graffito on an amphora fragment in Rome mentioned Beziers wine, five years old. Martial also notes a wine-merchant from Marseilles who had an office in Rome. This Munna smoked and doctored his wines and sold them in Italy for high prices comparable with those asked for the best Campanian Falernian. Munna never showed his face in Rome, scared, the poet comments, of having to drink his own brew.

In the late first century the Emperor Domitian, perturbed by the prospect of grain shortages after a year in which a poor harvest had been followed by a bumper vintage, and by the increasing use of good wheatlands for provincial vine-growing, especially in Gaul, issued an edict forbidding the planting of new vineyards and ordering the destruction of half of the existing vineyards in the provinces. This measure may also have been intended to protect the Italian wine trade. It is not clear how thoroughly it was carried out, in any case any vines destroyed would naturally have been the least productive ones.

By the second century important vineyards existed in Burgundy, south of Dijon between Nuits-St-Georges and Beaune. Lyons became an important distribution centre with a flourishing corporation of wine-merchants which put up a statue to a patron, M. Inthatius Vitalis, a citizen of Albi, who held a similar office among the shippers on the river Saône. In the south-west, wine-growing had spread down the Garonne probably assisted by new vines brought in from the Ebro region of Spain. By the third century vineyards had spread further along the Saône, and cellars are a not infrequent feature of dwellings in north-east Gaul. Lyons suffered from the defeat of Clodius Albinus by Septimius Severus in 297, and Trier inherited much of its importance as a trading centre. After the disastrous barbarian incursions of the third century the Emperor Probus in 277 is said to have rescinded Domitian's edict restricting the planting of vines, hoping to give the ravaged countryside a chance to regain its prosperity by vine-growing. Under Constantine in the early fourth century vineyards were flourishing between Beaune and Autun, and had spread along the Loire and the Seine. The Emperor Julian noted vineyards round Paris which produced a good wine.

Ausonius gives lyrical descriptions of vine-growing along the Moselle. A little evidence from sculpture and the discovery of vintner's knives suggest that the vine spread down the river and into the Rhineland by the end of the first century. The trenches of a vineyard of possible Roman date have been found close to a Roman settlement near Mayen. An inscription from Trier mentions a *cuparius*, a maker of the wooden casks used for Gallic wine. Trier was also a centre in the late second and early third centuries for the manufacture of clay drinking cups or beakers covered with a shiny black glaze and decorated with floral scrolls and mottoes in thick white paint. The mottoes are toasts for the drinkers, among them greetings such as, 'Hail, take me and be happy', 'Let us rejoice', 'Fill me up', 'Drink', 'Little water, undiluted wine'! Comments such as 'Hail, sweetness' and 'Love me, sweetheart' also occur, and fig. *59* illustrates a beaker with a picture of the goddess Minerva on one side. Such allusions prove that these vessels were filled with wine although some may have been used for beer drinking.

From the Danubian provinces the discovery of a primitive

59 Beaker showing Minerva. Trier

wine-press at a villa at Winden-am-See suggests that vines were being cultivated in Pannonia in the early second century. The bases of two other presses were found in different houses in Aquincum. Dio Cassius describes Pannonian wine as scarce and poor, but it may have been more plentiful after Probus's edict. There is also some evidence of experiments in wine-growing in Britain.

BRITISH FARMING COMMUNITIES

In Britain many of the inhabitants lived on isolated farms, in small family groups, or in larger villages in the well-drained areas of lighter soils in the south, such as the Sussex Downs. Many of these sites were occupied in pre-Roman times and life there continued with the minimum of disturbance, with some increase in size and a growing use of iron tools. Imported samian pottery was the chief luxury (see p. 176) and in some cases huts were replaced by more substantially constructed cottages. At Chisenbury Warren on the north-east of Salisbury Plain, aerial photographs show a settlement of 7 hectares (14½ acres) with turf platforms marking the whereabouts of 80 rectangular huts 12–18 m. (40–60 ft) long, ranged on both sides of a street. Much of the land outside the villages shows traces of ancient field systems.

In eastern England the Fenlands, previously almost unoccupied, seem to have been drained by the Roman administration. Here a large population settled in villages from late in the first century A.D.; the settlements flourished in the second and much of the third century, but the inhabitants were driven out by floods from this time onwards: the sea-level was rising and the administration for maintaining the drainage channels might have broken down so that by the fifth century the area reverted to its original marshy conditions. These villages were quite un-planned, straggling along the water-courses and surrounded by a few fields and gardens. In between are drove-roads and en-closures suggesting cattle-rearing on a large scale, probably for supplies of salted meat, lard, and hides for the army on the northern frontiers. It is possible that the Fens were an imperial estate, but no evidence for official administration of any kind has yet been found there.

A number of villas of varying size are also known in most parts of the country except the hillier areas of Cornwall, Wales and the North.

FARMING COMMUNITIES ELSEWHERE

In Gaul Caesar noted the existence of both single farms and villages and also mentioned the existence of 400 *vici* or villages among the Helvetii. Most of these must have been farming settlements. In the Trier area some may have existed along minor roads or in the more remote areas. In the Vosges near Sarrebourg, at Landscheid near Wittlich, and near Mayen, clusters of stone-built cottages have been found associated with ancient fields.

Along the Danube Hyginus, an official Roman surveyor, tells us about Pannonia, probably at the beginning of the second century. For tax purposes he divides the countryside into first- and second-class arable land, pasture, oak forest, and rough woods. Forest predominated. Much land was assigned to veterans or was attached to the fortresses and the towns. Even so, numbers of peasant communities tilling their own land existed along the Danube and in the more remote areas of Dalmatia and other provinces.

In the Near East land was also classified in various ways as mountain, hill or plain, good or bad, arable or forest, wet or dry or artifically irrigated; with soil of sand, clay or loam. The mid-fourth century author Libanius, a native of Antioch, gives us some glimpses of rural life in Syria and provides evidence for the existence of independent villages, inhabited by peasant pro-prietors. They may have held their land as communal owners, dividing it into strips and allocating so many strips to each farmer. At regular intervals the allocations were reviewed and the strips redistributed. Sometimes land was seized from another village, water-courses were diverted or trees cut down, and serious disputes resulted. Large, well-built villages discovered near Antioch probably owed much of their prosperity to the development of olive-plantations from the fourth century onwards. Village life went on with little contact with the towns, and the appearance of numerous peasants in Antioch on Easter Day was noted with interest by John Chrysostomus.

RURAL LIFE IN NORTH AFRICA

In Africa agriculture along the coast had flourished under Punic rule and after the Roman conquest Italian investors were anxious to buy land there. To acquire more territory for grain-growing, the Roman army fought its way far into the interior meeting strong opposition from the inhabitants, some of them desert nomads but others already accustomed to agricultural life. To begin with military posts were established to superintend such areas, some of the best land was acquired by immigrants, and the rest was reserved for the tribes to cultivate independently, subject to a tax of a certain proportion of their produce. In Tripolitania a number of inland farms have been identified on the hill slopes and valleys at the east end of the Gebel escarpment. The sites vary in size and include a few small villages. In some cases their well-built walls of local limestone masonry, often plastered and painted, still stand several feet high. None was fortified. Remains of many presses show that the majority were olive farms, but smaller quantities of other crops were also grown.

Africa was known above all as an area of large estates. As a result of either inheritance or confiscation much of this land passed into imperial control, but some continued in private ownership. Slave labour may have been used on certain estates, but elsewhere there were tenants. Thus in the second century we hear of workers living in villages, obliged to pay rent of about a third of their produce. Under the administration of either imperial procurators or bailiffs, large tracts of land might be leased out to contractors who could sublet or work land themselves with their own employees, aided by days of compulsory service from the tenants.

South of Carthage several imperial estates, administered from an estate office in Carthage, have been identified from inscriptions in the area near the Medjerda valley. This is hilly country first cleared and cultivated in Punic times, and native settlements already in existence were left undisturbed to provide a labour force. The oldest inscription dated to A.D. 116–7 comes from Henchir Mettich, south of the Medjerda valley and is addressed by two procurators to the tenants of the estate of Villa Magna Variana in the village of Siga. It refers to the Mancian law, a regulation probably made by one of the earlier private owers of the estate by which tenants were allowed to add any uncultivated and unassigned pieces of land to their holdings with security of tenure. Some of this land may have been in the hills away from the village. Apparently it was suitable for cereal cultivation since a special clause allows tenants to estimate the total yield of the crop and agree with the contractors on the proportion to be surrendered. This saved the tenant from having to cart the whole crop some distance for threshing and division. If the land was not cultivated for two years the tenancy ended. Apart from this special case the rent due from each tenant was the customary one-third and the products mentioned include wheat, barley, beans, figs, oil and wine, with a proportion of honey from each hive, five hives being the maximum permitted. (Presumably the contractors also kept bees and were afraid the swarms might be hived by the tenants.) When replanting of vines and fig-trees was necessary, taxation was remitted for five years. A small annual tax was due on sheep pastured on the estate. If a crop was robbed or destroyed, the tenant was still expected to pay the tax. He was also expected to give the estate two days' work at ploughing, at harvesting, and at cultivation, making six days' annual service.

In the reign of Commodus the tenants of the *Saltus Burunitanus* 'your rural workers, born and raised on your estates', sent a desperate petition to the Emperor complaining that the procurator in collusion with the contractors was demanding more rent and service than was due. When the tenants protested, soldiers had been sent to the estate and ill-treated them. An inscription found at Souk-el-Khmis records this petition and the Emperor's favourable reply, ordering that no more than six days' service be demanded from the tenants.

The names and probable locations of some privately-owned estates are known, among them those of Valeria Atticilla and the *Saltus Beguensis* belonging to Lucilius Africanus, neighbours in southern Tunisia. An inscription of A.D. 138 tells us that Africanus had obtained leave to hold market days twice a week at the *vicus Casae*, a village on his estate, provided that no disturbances resulted. Similar arrangements for the convenience of tenants are recorded from the estate of Antonia Saturnina. At harvest, fruit-picking and similar busy times, the labour forces of all estates might be augmented by gangs of men with little or no land of their own, who travelled around looking for extra work. The tombstone of one of them at Mactar records his career. His name has not survived, but from when he was a small child he worked on the land giving himself no rest. His parents were poor but he organized gangs of reapers around Cirta and elsewhere. After 21 years of hard frugal living he acquired his own house and land. Although originally a modest peasant, he was elected to the *ordo* and became a magistrate. He died a wealthy man after watching his children and grandchildren grow up around him, and describes his life as busy, peaceful and honoured by all. Another success story is that of Sicinius Aemilianus of Zarath. He belonged to a large family originally prosperous until the subdivision of its lands in plots among his relations left him with only one small field. Then an epidemic accounted for the rest of the family and the survivor found himself a wealthy man.

AFRICAN VILLAS

Pictures of the houses occupied by such estate owners appear on African mosaics, accompanied by scenes of rural life. One of the examples found at Tabarka shows a farm with barn and storage accommodation for the produce from the vines and olive trees depicted growing there, and also probably for the oil and wine presses, in front is the poultry yard. Other mosaics from the same site portray the stables with a fine horse nearby, and a shepherdess watching her sheep and spinning. Fig. 56 shows the owner's villa, built round a courtyard with look-out towers at each end and set in a park with trees and flowers, the haunt of pheasants and other wild birds. In the foreground a pond for ducks or fish appears. Agricultural scenes such as those on the second-century floors from a town house at Oudna(53) may depict life on the country estate which also belonged to the house owner, probably a city magistrate.

A mosaic from a villa on the coast near Sousse sums up the fertility of this part of Africa(60). In the centre is Neptune riding over the sea in his chariot attended by a Triton and a Nereid. In each corner is a Season. Winter, reed-crowned in a warm

60 Mosaic depicting the Fertility of Africa from a Tunisian villa

blue dress, holds two ducks suspended from a reed and is associated with olive growing (see p. 139). Spring, with a crown of flowers and a gold necklace, is framed in roses; her dog is tied to a rose branch and on her left is a rose-garden and a boy holding a flower basket. Summer, crowned with grain-ears, carries a basket and sickle, and is framed in grain; on her right is a lion in a grainfield and on her left a man reaping. Autumn, wreathed and framed in vines and grapes, is pouring out wine; on her right is a panther among vines and on her left a bearded man carries two baskets of grapes.

In Tripolitania there were also fine villas. Most of them are on the coast where the hot climate is alleviated by sea-breezes, and they tend to be within easy reach of towns. The large house at Dar Buk Ammera near Zliten is only a few miles from Lepcis. Built round a courtyard the north corridor had large windows with fine sea views and a mosaic floor. It faced out onto a terrace, probably a garden. The south corridor had a painted barrel-vaulted ceiling, the decoration of which fell onto the floor as the villa decayed; this has now been lifted and reconstructed. On one side is painted a delightful seaside village, the houses arranged in two rows with three or four a side(*61*); the inhabitants stroll around, mostly in pairs. The houses are two-storeyed with windows in the upper floor. A continuation of the same scene shows a woman waving to a ship in the bay; and trees and a purposeful dog also appear. Similarities to paintings from Pompeii and Stabiae date this work to the second half of the first century. The famous amphitheatre mosaic(*32*) and one depicting the seasons came from the living quarters. In contrast to the seaside villas there are the fortified inland farms found in large numbers in the eastern Gebel, especially along the Wadi Sofeggin. They were probably a late development occupied by more or less Romanized Libyans.

61   Wall-painting of a village. Zliten

EUROPEAN VILLAS

In the European provinces of the Empire the term 'villa' is used
for a whole range of country dwellings of various types. The
villa is an isolated farm depending on agriculture for a living.
At the lower end of the scale it may succeed on the same
site buildings of simple design and pre-Roman or early
Roman date, and reflect Roman influences on a native family by
such changes as the adoption of a rectangular plan, or a house
divided into several rooms. Building techniques improved, with
timber construction set on stone foundations to prevent rotting,
and thatch replaced by tiled or slated roofs. In some cases walls
are entirely of masonry. These modifications may be made by
members of a family who had lived on this land for some time, or
the land may be colonized by veterans or settlers from elsewhere.
Roman rule brought prosperity to many people and so some
villas grew in size, more rooms including baths were added, and
also refinements such as wall-paintings, mosaics, and gardens.
Other villas with less enterprising inmates changed little. At the
top end of the scale were the large estate owners with palatial
homes, rivalling or surpassing the town houses where they
presumably spent part of the year. Some owned several estates,
perhaps maintaining luxurious quarters in those they preferred
to visit, while on others only a dwelling for a bailiff, possibly
with simple accommodation for hunting parties, was required.
Families died out and villas decayed, perhaps when heiresses

married husbands with villas of their own. When there was competition for the imperial crown, supporters of the losing side often suffered confiscation of their property which might be treated as part of an imperial estate or resold.

If many individual factors make the study of Roman provincial villas difficult, they also make it fascinating, especially when modifications occur as a result of local conditions. Plans can be grouped under two very general headings: the peristyle house sometimes with an *atrium* (see below), with a plan recalling those of Italian villas or town houses; and the rest, houses, of varying size, the bigger ones with a large courtyard replacing the peristyle. One reason for these two groups is climate; the peristyle house was designed to keep out too much sunshine, while the others sought light and warmth and included rooms heated by hypocausts, in addition to the baths which were found in houses of both types. The absence or presence of pre-Roman farms of non-Italian type is another factor, and the gradual growth of a villa on a site with unlimited room for expansion might also encourage a less regimented lay-out.

Peristyle villas

The peristyle house is found in parts of Spain, with large wealthy houses like La Cocosa, near Badajoz, occupied from the mid-first century A.D. Here the entrance led straight into the peristyle with the family's rooms round it. Another group of buildings on one side housed the baths. Other blocks included kitchen, mill, storerooms and working quarters. Among the evidence for farming was a ploughshare and a wool comb.

In Southern France the peristyle house may have been inspired by town houses such as those at Vaison. South of Toulouse a large villa has been excavated at Montmaurin. Fig. *62* shows the partly reconstructed house at its most magnificent stage in the mid-fourth century. The entrance on the south through an imposing semi-circular court (at the top of fig. *62*) led into a large peristyle surrounded by the usual colonnades. The rooms on the right side of the peristyle include two of *atrium* plan open to the sky. In fact this side of the peristyle was occupied by a series of reception rooms with walls decorated with paintings or with marble wall veneers and mosaic floors. On the north side of the court a room with a wide entrance led into another peristyle of unusual form with three small water-basins on each side,

62   *Villa reconstruction. Montmaurin*

probably separated by panels of wall mosaic. Semicircular colonnades leading off it enclose small gardens. Next came a room at a higher level with a marble floor (in the foreground of fig. *62*); this was reached up steps and so looked down on to the court on one side and out into a small walled garden on the other. No doubt it was the family's private dining-room.

In the background on the right of fig. *62* can be seen part of a wing which contained the baths. These were reached by a corridor which passed on one side a shrine of the water nymphs in a paved court with a large water tank, and beyond it a small garden with a fountain. Near the house a number of farm buildings to accommodate workers and animals, tools and produce, have been found. An ice-house to store blocks of Pyrenean ice for use in hot weather is not unlikely.

Examples of the peristyle villa occur in Switzerland. Others are found occasionally in Bavaria and Romania, and there are several examples in Hungary. One recently excavated in Bulgaria near Ivailograd, not far from Adrianople, resembled Montmaurin in the extensive use of marble for decoration. A portrait of the owner with a small child on either side of him was worked into one of the mosaic floors. Somewhere in France the two different house plans constructed to avoid or encourage sun and light must overlap, and recent research suggests that examples of both styles may occur in Burgundy.

Other types of villa
The villas which developed in the cooler areas of the Empire have much humbler beginnings than the peristyle house.

In the west the classic example is the site at Mayen between Andernach and Coblenz in the Eifel near the lava quarries which provided the material for mill-stones traded widely in the north-western provinces. There a pre-Roman rectangular hut with timber posts supporting the roof, walls of wattle and daub and a central hearth, was rebuilt with dry stone walling at the beginning of the Roman period in the first century A.D. Traces of interior partitions may indicate that part of the space housed the farm animals. In front of this house was next built a corridor with a slated roof and a room at each end. At the end of the first century the house was rebuilt with masonry instead of dry stone walling (*63* top). The area of the ancestral hut remained in use as the main living-room with the hearth enlarged and retiled. The corridor had dwarf walls on which stood columns supporting its roof and the two rooms at each end were enlarged. A doorway from one of them led into three new rooms, the baths. Behind the house a tower granary was added. During the second century more rooms appeared on the other side of the house, and a cellar was dug under part of the corridor. Destruction followed during the third-century invasions but the house was rebuilt, only to be finally destroyed about a century later. Farm buildings, two shrines and an enclosure wall were also found at Mayen.

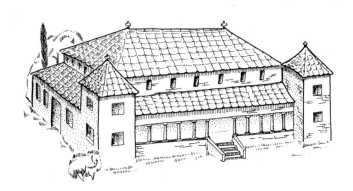

63   *Villa reconstructions.* top, *Mayen.* centre, *Vaesrade.* bottom, *Basse-Wavre*

Such development from pre-Roman beginnings and growth with increasing prosperity is typical of many villas. The house with front corridor is the most common type and widespread in both Europe and the Near East. The Mayen family seem to have been strongly conservative as they stuck to the plan with the large central living-room with hearth. Villas with this plan were particularly popular in Germany and must reflect a continuing tradition in which the hearth went on being the centre of domestic life, with cooking carried out there instead of in a separate kitchen. Even when the hearth disappears the large room remains.

Villas grew in size in various ways. Often a corridor was added behind the central rooms, Vaesrade in Holland is one example of this(63 centre); or, instead of a rear corridor, a second row of rooms was built. The Pannonian villa of Csucshegy in Hungary included a fine heated room in this area with an elaborate stucco ceiling, its decoration of small men, birds, leaves etc. arranged in geometric designs. Sometimes the villa considerably increased in length, and a well-known Belgian site at Basse-Wavre has over 40 rooms, including two short colonnades, spread out in three rows behind the front corridor(63 bottom). Alternatively more rooms were added at the corners forming wings. At Fliessem near Trier a villa built in the late second century had projecting wings and a wall cut off the house from a large enclosure with farm buildings. In this way the villa owner had a more secluded garden or courtyard away from the estate activities, such courtyards surrounded by rooms on two or three sides are a feature of the larger houses.

Out-buildings

As we have seen, villas are often accompanied by various other structures. On the outskirts of Cologne one has been found looking out on to a garden and orchards, with family graves just inside the wall which encloses the whole establishment(64), and a larger cemetery for the workers outside. Elaborate wall-paintings decorated some of its rooms with dados imitating the marble wall veneers of wealthier villa-owners. Moulds and traces of bronze-working suggest that craftsmen were at work in a small building near one end of the house. Behind this was a large barn with the customary wide entrance. Near the other end of the house was a cellar with another store behind. Behind the villa was a small

64   *Reconstruction. The villa at Cologne-Mungersdorf. Farm-buildings in the foreground, dwelling house in the centre with garden and orchards behind. Burials in enclosures, top right-hand corner*

house with a corridor, perhaps providing living accommodation for the farm workers. The other buildings are byres, sheep-folds and pig-sties, and a large stable with a tower granary or hayloft. It is suggested that the farm stock included 20 horses and 30 cattle.

In some cases, notably in Belgium, the estate workers were not only occupied with farming. At Anthée near Namur a fine large house stands at the back of its own extensive courtyard at one end of a large oblong enclosure, from which it is cut off by the usual wall. Parallel to the walls of the main enclosure are 20 small buildings in two carefully planned rows. Some are indeed agricultural but others have furnaces and hearths for iron- and bronze-working and enamelling. Evidence was found for a variety of iron implements, bronze jewellery, weights, decorative appliqués, and ornaments for the harness made by the leather-workers in another building. The finished articles were stored in cellars until they were sent to market. Other sites of this kind no doubt existed.

7

Communications and trade

By the time of the Emperor Diocletian, Rome had built 85,000 km. (53,000 miles) of roads linking it with the most distant provinces(65). Most of them were constructed in the first two centuries of our era and little practical information about them can be gained from literary sources. The poet Statius, however, writing about A.D. 90, describes the work on a road built in Campania by Domitian. Its course was marked out by trenches and then the area between them dug out and filled in with slabs of stone set in mortar, often above a layer of sand. Above came concrete with crushed stone and mortar and a surface of stone slabs, often of polygonal shape. The resulting road-bed might be 100–140 cm. (40–55 in.) thick. It would endure for years without repair. Drainage ditches were constructed on both sides and stone curbs might separate carriage-ways from the ditches and sidewalks. Marshy areas were crossed on wooden causeways, steep slopes were sometimes negotiated with zig-zags, and the mountains were pierced by tunnels.

In the provinces the fully paved roads tend to be found in or near cities where the mud or dust produced by other surfaces would be obnoxious(66). Elsewhere cobbles or a gravel surface on a gravel or rammed-stone foundation is found, with by-roads with just a thin skin of gravel on natural soil. The construction varied with the materials available locally. Main roads might be up to 12 m. (40 ft) wide although not all this area would be paved. Other roads vary between 3–6 m. (10–20 ft) in width.

The straightness of Roman roads is proverbial but in actual fact they are made up of a series of straight alignments which indicate the distance from one sighting mark to the next, with the routes not necessarily taking the most direct way. Individual sections change direction gradually to fit in with the terrain. The army's expert surveyors had to plot the course of roads through

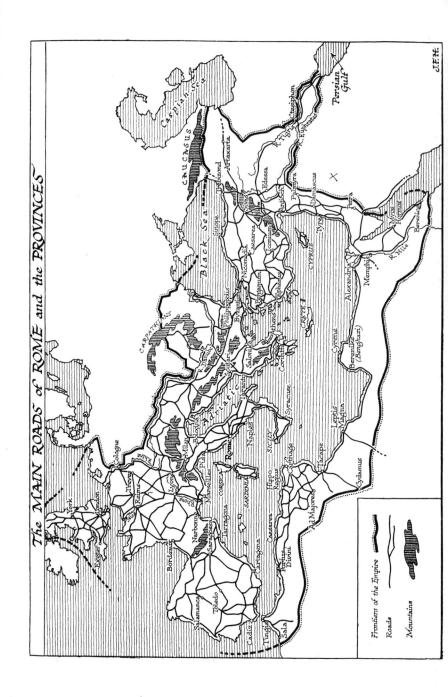

The MAIN ROADS of ROME and the PROVINCES

66   Paved road built by Trajan on the way to Antioch

new and often hostile territory. Sometimes they may have been helped by local information, occasionally they followed earlier roads or trackways, otherwise scouting parties must have gone ahead to explore the way.

MAPS

Initially, little help was available from maps. Agrippa planned and Augustus set up in Rome a large sculptured chart of the Roman world which was probably copied elsewhere. The land surveyors are known to have made maps in duplicate on sheets of bronze, one copy going to the record office in Rome, the other kept locally. The Peutinger Table, a twelfth-century copy probably based on a third-century map of the world from Britain to India shows some cities, roads and distances, although with topographical distortions. The *Notitia Dignitatum*, a list of officials in the late Empire, was provided with somewhat inadequate maps.

Soldiers and travellers may have carried lists of places and the distances between them. The Antonine Itinerary comprises some 225 routes of this kind believed to have been originally compiled

67 *The Tongres Itinerary*

for the actual or projected journeys of the Emperor Caracalla, with careful note taken of the cities where supplies could be obtained. Some of the routes are later accretions, perhaps for troop movements or official journeys. The Ravenna Cosmography, surviving as a seventh-century list based on earlier material, confirms parts of the Antonine Itinerary and with these sources and inscriptions it has been possible to identify many town names and the distances between them.

In some cases columns were erected on which lists of towns lying along the main roads were carved. One in Rome gave the distances to all the major cities of the Empire. Part of a hexagonal column of this type survives from Tongres, a city along the important road from Cologne to Boulogne probably built by Claudius for the invasion of Britain (67). On the right of its three sides the distances to Cassel near the Belgian coast, Fines Atrebatum (probably Bethune), Arras and Bavai are given. In the centre the directions pick up a road from Cologne to Amiens. The other side mentions a German road beside the Rhine going south from Bonn, to Mainz and Worms. The names and distances largely agree with those given in the Peutinger Table and correct some details of the Antonine Itinerary.

ROAD CONSTRUCTION

The main roads were largely built by the army especially in new provinces, and paid for by the state, often with war booty. Emperors, generals or rich individuals spent large sums on road-building and were rewarded with statues or other memorials. Slaves, prisoners and even gladiators assisted in the work. Cities financed work in their vicinity with customs duties and tolls, and from the third century onwards were usually responsible for all expenses. By this time few new roads were needed and alterations and repairs were the major problems. In the country villa-owners and villages paid for their local roads.

The earliest road built outside Italy was the Via Egnatia in Dalmatia which was started in 148 B.C. Traffic came down the Via Appia to near Brindisi and was shipped across the Adriatic to Durazzo. It went over the mountains of Albania to Pella in Macedonia and Salonika on the Aegean Sea. By the time of Nero the road of 864 km. (540 miles) ended at Istanbul (Byzantium) on the Black Sea. Under Hadrian this road was extended along the coast to Tomi in Romania.

The road from Rome to Cadiz opened up Southern France for Romanization. Lyons became a major centre from which a network of roads stretching to the Atlantic Ocean, the Channel and the North Sea was built by Claudius, Vespasian and Trajan. In Britain after Claudius's invasion London became the major road centre, and a similar network developed all over England and Wales as far north as the Scottish Highlands.

From Aquileia and northern Italy roads led north through Austria and Germany to the Danube and Rhine. Problems with the marshy country of the Rhine delta were solved by adapting the native plank roads laid on bundles of brushwood, improving their drainage and surfacing them with sand and gravel. By Trajan's reign a road 1,600 km (1,000 miles) long ran from Holland along the Rhine and Danube to Tomi via Vienna and Belgrade.

In North Africa the characteristic network is found extending inland from Carthage, covering the area north of the road linking Gabes and Algiers. Other roads ran south linking the desert trade with ports. One led through the rich olive plantations of the eastern Gebel and enabled the oil to be brought to the harbour at Lepcis. Outside many Roman cities the roads are mere tracks, levelled and cleared of boulders, and in much of Africa the dry soil and underlying rock can carry traffic without further modification. Eventually a coast road 4,480 km. (2,800 miles) long ran from Tangiers to Alexandria. From Alexandria it continued into Israel and Lebanon. Trajan extended it to Antioch and along the coast to Asia Minor, alongside the Hellespont and the Sea of Marmora to the southern side of the Bosphorus. A network of other major roads covered the interior of Asia Minor.

Milestones

The line of the roads was marked by milestones every 1,000 paces, a Roman mile (1,481 m.: 4,833 ft). Usually cylindrical columns, they were inscribed with the reigning emperor's name and titles and the distance from the nearest town (*68*). When the town or the mileage is missing, it is presumed that these details were added in paint. In Gaul and the Rhineland a Celtic measurement, the league of *c.* 2,220–2,430 m. was often used instead of the mile, and this is the measurement indicated by the abbreviation L on the Tongres inscription (*67*).

When road repairs were performed, new milestones were set up recording the work. The Via Augusta in Spain 'from Tarragona to Cadiz was built by Augustus and repaired in places by Caligula, Claudius and Nero. Vespasian in A.D. 79 ordered more work on it and built some new bridges and restored old ones, but eleven years later repairs were again necessary under his son Domitian. At the end of the century Trajan rebuilt and restored Spanish roads which were worn out with long use. The Via Augusta certainly attracted heavy civilian traffic and Trajan's work must have been thoroughly carried out, as little more seems to have been done until A.D. 214. Then Caracalla, aware of the bad state of the roads in many parts of the Empire, organized extensive repairs. An inscription of Valentinian I in 364 records that Spanish roads worn out by long use were restored to their original excellence, and a fourth-century milestone notes

68 Carriage approaching a milestone, Trier

the restoration of a road over the Pyrenees which had been completely destroyed by a flood.

Bridges

While shallow water could be forded, and paved fords to assist the traveller do exist in some places, the roads crossed most rivers on bridges. The Romans were great bridge-builders and their structures varied from clapper bridges consisting of one or two slabs over brooks to imposing constructions in wood or stone, or the two combined. Only fragments of the stone piers remain of the greatest, Trajan's bridge over the Danube in Romania built by Apollodorus of Damascus. It appears on Trajan's column and had 20 piers, each 39 m. (100 ft) high and 19 m. (60 ft) wide, 52 m. (170 ft) apart. These carried a wooden bridge with a balustrade. In Portugal, Apollodorus built a stone bridge 220 m. (728 ft) long, on 18 arches over the Upper Tagus. Little of this survives, but another famous stone bridge over the Tagus can still be seen at Alcantara(69). It links Spain and Portugal and was built about A.D. 104 by the architect C. Julius Lacer and paid for by eleven towns in the neighbourhood. Above the centre of the bridge a triumphal arch was created in honour of Trajan. On the Portuguese bank the same architect built a small temple which still survives, and which is dedicated to Trajan and the Gods for help received in work which would last for centuries.

The bridge across the Rhine which linked Mainz and Castel appears on a Roman medallion found at Lyons(70). Excavation has shown that its piers stood on a foundation of wooden piles, their tips protected by iron shoes. On one side the piers were built

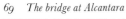

69   The bridge at Alcantara

70 Silver medallion from Lyons showing the bridge at Mainz

out in triangular plan to break the force of the current. This was a favourite device of Roman architects. The stones of the piers were bound together by iron cramps and supported a timber bridge.

TRAVELLERS ON THE ROADS

Besides the army and civilian travellers the roads were used by the couriers of the *cursus publicus*, a system organized by Augustus by which dispatches could be speedily conveyed to officials anywhere in the Empire. It depended upon relays of horses being always in readiness at distances of 10–20 km. (6–16 miles) apart, according to the nature of the country, for messengers on horseback or in carriages. Grooms and wheelwrights had to be provided, and every 30 to 40 km. (20–25 miles), an inn for overnight stops. Local communities had to pay for these supplies and complained bitterly. The couriers could cover 80 km. (50 miles) in 24 hours. High officials and their families could also use the facilities but they needed special passes to do so. A limited number of these passes was issued by the governors in each province. A slower service of ox-wagons covering 13–15 km. (8–9½ miles) a day brought official supplies and baggage.

Sometimes the inns for travellers were in cities but many of them were built by the roadside and often villages or even towns developed around them. One recently excavated at Chameleux in Belgium on the road from Rheims to Trier is typical of its kind(*71*). Built in the first century, it was altered and reconstructed several times after accidental fires and flooding. Rebuilding always followed on the same site. Buildings were found on either side of the road and the largest one had a court with a gate wide enough for the entrance of the carriages and wagons. Stables and the inn were ranged round it. A large cellar down a wooden staircase had a sanded floor and oak supports to keep

71 Reconstruction. The settlement at Chameleux. The inn is at the end of the street on the left

upright a number of wine-jars. A forge repaired harness and made horse-shoes. In the troubled times following the third-century invasions some road stations were fortified. The inhabitants of Chameleux, however, seem to have sought refuge on the nearby hilltop of Williers, from about the beginning of the fourth century.

VEHICLES

Pack animals were used(72), and a mule would carry up to 150 kilos (330 lbs). Wheeled transport included wagons with two or four solid or spoked wheels. One, known as the *plaustrum*, appears on the silver cup from Castro Urdiales(73); the large barrel on its platform is being filled with water from the healing spring. Sometimes this cart might have high sides, and one like it filled with wine-skins appears on a mosaic dating from the end of the third century from a house in New Paphos, Cyprus.

For fast journeys the *cisium*, a light two-wheeled carriage drawn by one or two ponies or mules was used. One with two passengers appears passing a milestone on the Igel monument, and a man drives a double team on a relief from Gherla, Hungary. The four-wheeled variety, probably called the *raeda*, appears on a tombstone from Moesia, now in a Belgrade museum; here it is drawn by three horses and is transporting L. Blassius Nigellio, a courier of the *cursus publicus*, who sits behind the driver holding a scroll, his urgent despatch, and behind him is his servant with the luggage. The *raeda* could also convey up to 330 kilos (722 lbs) drawn by eight or ten mules. Ox-wagons could carry 429 kilos (944 lbs). Passengers also travelled in

72 *Bronze statuette of a donkey.*
British Museum

73 *Silver bowl, Castro Urdiales*

carriages covered with awnings or with coach-like bodies. A well-known example of the latter, from Klagenfurt in Austria, may have been used for sleeping.

The horse was chiefly used for riding and to pull light carriages, and fine harness and carriage trappings are often indicated on tombstones. Saddles were strapped on over colourful saddle-cloths sometimes decorated with fringe. Stirrups were not used but prick spurs are found occasionally, mostly on military sites. Iron horse and mule shoes were used on paved roads.

WATER TRANSPORT

While road and bridge building were the great Roman contributions to improved communications, land transport was slow and expensive. Diocletian's edict tells us that in the fourth century a wagon carrying 500 kilos (1,100 lbs) cost up to 20 denarii a mile and a donkey load cost four. So a wagon-load of grain bought for 6,000 denarii would double its price by the time it had travelled 300 miles.

For cheapness and comfort water travel was greatly preferable and pre-Roman routes up rivers, along coasts, and across narrow seas such as the Channel were exploited to the full. The Atlantic and North Sea were not as attractive to travellers of Mediterreanean origin, and sailors and the majority of passengers in these areas tended to be Celts and Germans who were more accustomed to local conditions.

The army used water transport as far as possible to provision forts and fortresses, many of which had their own small river harbours. Most of the traffic on the Danube, Drave and Save was military rather than commercial, except in the upper reaches of the Danube which had links with Germany and north Italy, and river ports at Vindobona, Aquincum etc. In Spain the Guadalquivir (Baetis) was navigable by sea-going ships as far as Seville, smaller ships could continue a little further north, but after that only river-boats could get up to Cordoba. From there the river is. no longer navigable. Traces of a quay with a fine building with columns have been found at Seville. A special official (*procurator Baetis*) was entrusted with seeing that the river was dredged and remained navigable.

In Gaul river traffic was of major importance. Along the Atlantic coast the Garonne, Durance, Loire and Seine took barges into the interior. The sea-going vessels could sail up the Rhône as far as Arles, then their cargoes travelled on in river-boats to Vienne and Lyons. From there they might go on to Geneva or proceed up the Saône to Chalons. Traces of quays have been found at both. From Chalons traffic went overland to the Seine or Loire, or to the Moselle. and Rhine.

We owe our best description of a river in Roman times to Ausonius who described a journey up the Moselle from Coblenz in the fourth century. As far as Berncastel the river flowed through pathless forest. Then he came to Neumagen, an important road centre, and open country with the roofs of farmhouses appearing on the hills which were green with vines. The river here flowed steadily along, and shells, waterweed and many varieties of fish could be seen in its crytal clear water. The salmon and perch are noted with particular appreciation. On the slopes the farmworkers and vine-dressers exchanged boisterous jests with the wayfarers tramping along the bank or the bargemen floating by. At one place boys in small rowing boats raced and played, elsewhere fishermen were busy. The courts and colonnades of splendid villas appeared as the river neared Trier, some on the slopes, others on its banks, one with a fish-pool made by constructing a weir.

NAUTAE

River traffic was organized by the *nautae*, wealthy guilds of merchant shippers. Many inscriptions relating to their activities have been found at Lyons. A dedication survives from a monument put up in honour of his colleagues by C. Julius Sabinianus. The corporation of Rhône *nautae*, to which they all belonged, gave the land by decree and each one was given 3 denarii when the monument was dedicated. Other Lyons shippers belonged to the Saône corporation. Some are described as oil, wine, or grain merchants as well. Others belonged to the guilds of both the Rhône and the Saône. A fragment of a relief of a Saône shipper found at Dijon shows that this guild was also concerned with the land transport necessary to link its cargoes with other rivers at this point; below the inscription a man appears loading a wagon.

Nautae are recorded from the river Seine at Paris and the Moselle at Metz. Several from the Rhine include Blussus, aged 75 and his wife Menimane, whose first-century tombstone was put up by their son Primus(*74*). Both are wearing native costume (see p. 106). Menimane has her pet dog on her knee while Blussus clutches one of his money bags. On the back of the tombstone is a boat containing several men; a small mast for a tow-rope rather

than a sail is a reminder that many of the river boats were barges, to be rowed or hauled upstream. Ausonius notes the bargemen struggling against the current in one direction and floating easily with it in the other, and they appear on a relief from Cabrières-d'Aigues near Avignon towing a boat laden with wine barrels, below a row of amphorae and glass flagons encased in wicker-work. Moselle boats laden with barrels and decorated with animal figure-heads also appear on the Igel monument (see *103*

74   Relief of Blussus and Menimane, Mainz

below p. 217). Besides the *nautae* there were other important guilds of boatmen including hauliers, raftmen and also
shipwrights.

NAVICULARII

There were also guilds of ship-owners and merchants, the
navicularii, who organized sea transport. Originally independent,
their responsibility for getting the vital grain supplies to Italy led
to increasing regimentation until they really became a state
service. In the first and second centuries, however, private
enterprise could still take advantage of growing prosperity.
Inscriptions mentioning them occur at Narbonne, while at Arles
they were gathered into at least five corporations. The best
impression of their activities however, is gained from the mosaics
which lie outside the numerous small rooms of the Piazzale delle
Corporazione at Ostia. These seem to have been the Italian
offices of *navicularii* from many parts of the Empire. The
Narbonne guild is represented there and so is Arles with a mosaic
showing its pontoon bridge over the rivers which meet in the
estuary of the Rhône. The elephant on the mosaic of the
Sabrathan guild may be an allusion to Africa's ivory exports.
Other mosaics depicting animals may indicate firms shipping
exhibits for the amphitheatre sports.

Guilds of shipwrights also existed at the major ports. At Arles,
a member of one of them, Caecilius Niger, was buried on the
banks of the Rhône near the shipyards, and a second-century
marble tablet describes Coelius D . . . as a naval architect.
Diocletian's edict discriminates between the builders of sea-going
and of river boats, the former being paid 60 denarii a day which
was ten more than the latter.

RIVER AND SEA CRAFT

A mosaic in the cold bath of a fine house at Medeina (Althiburos)
in Tunisia shows a variety of river and sea-going boats with their
names and an occasional poetic quotation. The river craft
include types seen on the reliefs from Mainz and Cabrières
d'Aigues. There is also a ferry-boat loaded with three horses,
named Ferox, Icarus, and Cupido. The sea-going ships include
the most common varieties, the *ponto* and the *corbita*. The keel of
the *ponto* projected in front of the stern post like a battleship's

75   *Relief of a ship. Sidon*

ram; possibly this was for added strength when the ship was beached. A second- or third-century mosaic from Tebessa shows one somewhat overladen with amphorae, with its sails down and the oars in action. The ship is guided by two large steering paddles on either side of the stern. Similar boats sometimes used for fishing appear on other African mosaics in the Bardo Museum, Tunis. Underwater archaeologists are recovering a series of wrecks from the waters of the Mediterranean, several of them with cargoes of amphorae. Overloading seems to have been a frequent cause of disaster.

The graceful *corbita* had a rounded hull from which stem and stern rose in gentle curves. The best picture of one comes from a tomb at Sidon, where it is shown floating away on its last voyage on a sea full of fish and leaping dolphins. The sails are set and the swan figure-head and the steering paddles are clearly shown (75).

JOURNEYS BY SEA

Little is known of the seafarers and travellers who journeyed in these ships. At Salona in Yugoslavia there is a portrait of C. Utius who made many journeys by land and sea. On his tombstone is a *corbita*, its sails furled. In the second half of the second century the Greek poet Lucian described a grain-ship from Egypt called the *Isis Geminiana* which was driven off its course by bad weather for 70 days until it docked at the port of Piraeus to recover. It was 54 m. (177 ft) long, with flame-coloured sails, and an anchor with windlass and capstan. The steersman was named Hero, bald but for a curly fringe, and his ship carried enough grain to feed Athens for a year. Lionel Casson has calculated that the *Isis* would have been about 1228 tons, the size of Nelson's *Victory*. After leaving Alexandria she reached Cyprus in seven days but unusually severe summer gales forced her off course to Sidon. Eventually she worked along the coasts of Syria and Asia Minor, narrowly escaping running aground. From Piraeus she would go on past Malta and Sicily to discharge her cargo at Puteoli. The voyage back from Puteoli to Alexandria would be helped by the prevailing winds and would last 20–25 days. Speed at sea varied from about four to six knots, depending on the wind and on whether the voyage was in open waters or hugging the coasts. In bad weather only two knots might be possible. From various literary sources it has been calculated that voyages from Rome to Carthage took $4\frac{1}{2}$–$6\frac{1}{2}$ days, to Marseilles 1–$1\frac{1}{2}$, and to Narbonne 3. From Ostia or Carthage to Gibraltar both took 7 days, Corinth to Puteoli $4\frac{1}{2}$.

Propitiating the gods

Travellers took care to propitiate the gods with vows of new altars should they arrive safely at their destinations. At Bordeaux, M. Aurelius Lunaris, priest of the imperial cult at both Lincoln and York (see p. 188), dedicated an altar to his tutelary goddess Boudiga with a river god on one side depicting either the Garonne or the Ouse. He was probably a wine-merchant. A Chester tombstone in memory of a soldier who died in a shipwreck while awaiting promotion to the rank of centurion is a reminder of the dangers of sea-travel.

No one was more aware of this than the merchants trading with Britain across the North Sea. At Domburg on the Isle of Walcheren and at Colijnsplaat on the bank of the East Scheldt were two temples of the goddess Nehalennia who watched over these traders during the prosperous years of the second and early third centuries. Towards the end of this period she was defeated by the elements herself as both her temples were swallowed up by the sea.

In 1970 fragments of altars were found in fishermen's nets near Colijnsplaat, and a wonderful collection of over a hundred have now been dredged up there. Usually they bear a relief of Nehalennia as a seated mother-goddess holding a basket of fruit and with her dog beside her. Alternatively she may appear as a

76 *Relief of Nehalennia. Colijnsplaat*

younger woman, standing, her foot on the prow of a ship. The altar (76), was dedicated to her by Marcus Exgingius Agricola, a citizen of Trier and a salt merchant from Cologne. Two more salt merchants appear on other altars. It is difficult to decide in which direction the salt was travelling as salterns exist on both sides of the North Sea. Two more altars were put up by traders in *allec*, another name for *garum*, the ubiquitous Roman fish sauce. Brought north from the Mediterranean this must have been a cargo for Britain, a hint that Romanized cooks were at work there. Elsewhere M. Secundinius Silvanus gives thanks for the safe passage of his merchandise, a load of pottery. A fragment showing a boat laden with wine-barrels survives from another altar, and one dedication was made by a father anxious for his son's welfare.

Ports and harbours
Outside Italy our knowledge of harbours is very limited although underwater archaeology is now contributing much fresh information.

In western Anatolia, Miletus had been an important commercial centre since Greek times. It had four harbours, the chief
one an inlet on the north with a narrow entrance which could be
closed with a chain. On either side two stone lions of Hellenistic
date kept guard. Marble-paved quays surrounded the inlet on
three sides with a colonnade with 30 shops on the south side. At
the east end a fine Roman gateway led to the road to the city
centre. A monument depicting a ship, probably erected in
honour of Augustus, was decorated with reliefs of sea-gods. With
the silting up of the harbour Miletus's prosperity declined.
Further south, silt made the harbour at Caunos increasingly
hazardous so that foreign traders ceased to call there. An
inscription concerned with customs duties shows that in the first
century A.D. many duties were remitted in an effort to attract
trade, and some of the citizens gave 60,000 denarii to meet the
deficit.

Many harbours of varying importance have been identified on
the coast of North Africa. Between Alexandria and Carthage,
sheltered inlets are few, but at Lepcis Magna the estuary of the
Wadi Lebda, protected on the north and east by outlying reefs,
provided a haven. Quays were built beside the estuary and under
Septimius Severus massive masonry moles were built, enclosing
the harbour on the north and east(77). To prevent periodic
flooding the Lebda was dammed and provided with a new
channel to the south-west of the city. The moles were stepped
back from the water on two or three levels. Ships were berthed

77   East harbour mole, Lepcis Magna

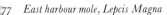

against the lowest one, the rear wall of which has projecting stones pierced with holes for mooring ropes. Ramps or flights of steps led up to the higher levels.

At the end of the north mole another stretch ran out north-eastwards. On the end of this was the lighthouse two storeys high, built on a square platform a little above sea-level. The form taken by the lantern on top is uncertain. The whole building was probably between 30 and 35 m. (98 and 114 ft) high. A smaller tower on the end of the east mole may have been used for signalling. Near it was a masonry structure 2 m. (6½ ft) high to which the chain closing the harbour was probably attached.

Lighthouses

Early mariners may have been guided by beacons lit on hill-tops. The famous Pharos of Alexandria built about 280 B.C. is the earliest known lighthouse and the fire lit on top of it was reflected by mirrors of polished metal. The Roman lighthouse at the mouth of the Tiber at Portus, four storeys high, appears on coins, reliefs, and mosaics, and others are known to have existed round the Mediterranean at Capri, Fréjus in France and Caepio and Corunna in Spain. The Corunna example, the much restored Torre de Hercules, was built in the second century A.D. by C. Servius Lupus, with a dedication to Mars. Strabo describes Caepio as resembling the Alexandrian Pharos. It warned ships of sunken rocks and shallows at the mouth of the Gualdalquivir. On the Channel coast Suetonius tells us Caligula erected a high tower with a beacon to guide ships at Boulogne, and this survived until the sixteenth century. It is said to have been octagonal with 12 storeys 60 m. (196 ft) high. Across the sea two lighthouses must have signalled back on either side of the harbour at Dover. A substantial portion of the eastern one survives.

CAMEL CARAVANS

Another method of transport found in the East and in North Africa was the camel-caravan. While the camel with two humps was at home in the deserts and mountains from Iran to the Gobi, the single humped dromedary was used in Arabia, probably spreading from there into Egypt and across North Africa, perhaps by the end of the first century A.D. The desert tribes also adopted it, and in drier areas where other animals were scarce, it was used for ploughing. Terracotta statuettes of dromedaries from

78   Clay model of a camel, Aphrodisias

Egypt show them laden with baskets of grapes or with wine jars fitted on either side of a heavy pack-saddle. A statuette from Aphrodisias in Asia Minor shows the driver perched on the back of a kneeling camel with a large amphora on one side balanced by a sheep on the other(*78*). Diocletian's edict prices a camel-load of 250 kilos (600 lbs) at 8 denarii a mile.

Several caravan routes crossed Arabia by the Nile Delta to the Arabian Sea, one with much traffic starting at Arsinoë at the head of the Gulf of Suez and ending at Gerrha on the Persian Gulf. Syria had been the centre where east and west met from remote antiquity, and another desert route led north from Egypt to Petra. Petra was the meeting place for caravans from Gerrha or from Charax Spasinu at the head of the Persian Gulf. So heavy was the traffic here bringing perfumes and spices that Strabo compared it to an army.

Continuing north from Petra travellers would reach Damascus on the route from the port at Tyre to the fertile oasis of Palmyra, and travel east to Dura-Europos on the Euphrates. In April 193, a statue was put up in Palmyra in honour of Thaimarsas, a caravan leader; it was erected by the men whom he led on the journey from Charax Spasinu to Palmyra and who wished to recognize his kindness to them and his contribution of 300 denarii for expenses, and to honour his sons Jaddaius and Jabdibolus.

TRADE WITH THE EAST AND WITH AFRICA

From the Tigris and Euphrates travellers went on by land or sea on journeys which sometimes ended only in China, Malaysia or India. From Chinese traders was obtained the silk spun for the tunics of luxurious Roman ladies on the looms at Tyre and Beirut. From India came ebony and teak, rice, diamonds, and other precious stones and many spices, notably pepper and ginger. In return Rome sent wine, glass, copper, tin and lead, and Arretine pottery. Several travellers' records survive of such journeys. The discovery of the periodicity of the monsoon winds by the sailor, Hippalus, in the mid-first century A.D. enabled ships to travel across the sea without hugging the coast. It became possible to leave Egypt in July, reach India in November, and sail back with the north-east monsoon at the end of November, reaching Alexandria in February.

African trade was carried on with Ethiopia and Central Africa from ports such as Lepcis Magna. In A.D. 202 an inscription listing customs duties was set up at the inland town of Zarai (Algeria) on the boundary between Numidia and Mauretania. Animals for the local market were duty-free but otherwise dues demanded include $1\frac{1}{2}$ denarii on a slave worth 500, and on horses and mules worth 400, and a duty of about 2 per cent on tunics, blankets, cloaks and tablecloths and $2\frac{1}{2}$ per cent on wine, *garum*, dates and figs. In exchange for these items Zarai obtained salt, flax, iron and copper. Cargoes passing Coptos, an important port on the Nile connected with the Red Sea, had to pay a toll of 8 drachmas for each captain of a Red Sea ship, 5 for a sailor, 1 for a man returning from a long voyage, 20 for army wives or women arriving by sea, 108 for courtesans, one obol for a camel, 2 for an ass, 20 drachmas for a mast and 1 drachma 4 obols for a return fare for a funeral.

POTTERY

Fragments of both locally-made or imported pottery vessels are often found in tombs or during excavations and the study of the various types sheds much light on trading activities. Kilns supplying local needs occurred frequently outside towns, in smaller settlements or even near villas. Amphorae for wine and oil stamped with the trader's name had a much wider distribution: a huge pile of fragments found in Rome, for example, mostly came from Spanish suppliers. The most useful pottery for tracing trade contacts, however, is the red-gloss samian ware which found its way all over the Empire to the dinner tables of all but the very poorest. Tough and distinctive, it was treasured, and if it got broken was lovingly repaired with lead rivets. The siting of the potteries was determined by the availability of suitable clays. Each centre included several workshops run by individual potters, and in Italy and western Europe these potters each stamped their names on their pots. They did this partly because several craftsmen shared a kiln so it was necessary for each to identify his own property, partly as a check on individual workers, and partly for advertisement.

The manufacture of Roman red-gloss ware began with the fine pottery made at Arezzo and a few other minor Italian sites in the first century B.C. About A.D. 10 pottery inspired by this Arretine ware began to be made in southern Gaul east of Toulouse. At La Graufesenque a large centre with several hundred potters grew up. Sometimes lists, possibly of pots being fired together, were incised on plates and from these records and lists of stamps we know that many of the craftsmen were Gauls. One called Tritos made more than 150,000 pots. Unlike Arezzo where the workers were slaves, the provincial potters were probably free men. Their decorated pottery includes bowls ornamented in relief with vegetation and some figures of men or animals. Pottery from southern Gaul was sold all round the Mediterranean.

By the mid-first century another group of potteries making red gloss ware had started work round Clermont-Ferrand. Lezoux was the most important, and towards the end of the second century its products were in use in quantity in France, Britain, Holland, Belgium, the Rhineland, Switzerland and along the banks of the Danube. The Italian potteries had declined owing to Gaulish competition, and a packing case full of Lezoux ware was buried at Pompeii in the eruption of A.D. 79. The typical bowl is decorated with mythological or hunting scenes. Fig. *79g* shows a design with the stamp of Paternus in relief back to front among the decoration while C. Albinus has impressed his mark on the rim.

The central Gaulish potteries ceased production at the end of the second century. No one knows why. It may be that the potters were conscripted to fight for Albinus and when he was defeated by Septimius Severus, the local merchants may have shared in his ruin. But new samian potteries developed in east Gaul and in the Rhineland at Trier and Rheinzabern(*79d,e*). Probably they were started by potters from central Gaul. Distribution was confined to the northern provinces and disrupted by the mid third-century invasions. Samian was also made in Spain and at

Aquincum and Colchester. The chief rival of the Gaulish pottery, however, was the North African red ware made of coarser clay. Its types were limited but they included dishes and casseroles with lids(*79a-c*). Few cups and jugs were found; presumably cheap glass replaced them. The chief centres of production were in Tunisia round Carthage and El Djem, close to the sea for the convenience of the enormous export trade. With the exception of Egypt, all North Africa, Italy, Sicily, Dalmatia and Greece were using this pottery by the second century. By the third and fourth centuries the trade expanded to the Mediterranean coasts of France and Spain, Egypt and Syria.

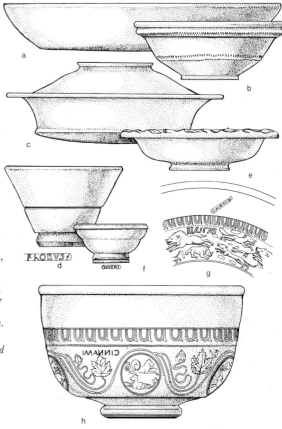

79 Pottery. a–c, *North African red ware.* a, *Athens.* b, *Germa.* c, *Tripoli.* d–h, *samian ware.* d, *cup with stamp of Florus, Niederbieber.* e, *dish from Pfunz.* f, *cup with stamp of Quintanus, Aislingen.* g, *Lezoux bowl with stamps of Albinus and Paternus, Lakenheath.* h, *Lezoux bowl with stamp of Cinnamus, Auvergne*

178

GLASS

Among the most beautiful objects from the Roman Empire still in existence are the glass vessels. Their survival, which often seems little short of miraculous, is largely due to the custom of including them as funeral offerings, sometimes as cinerary urns, protected by coffins or other containers. A stone coffin found at Beauvais contains a woman's skeleton accompanied by no fewer than ten jugs and beakers. Probably her family owned a glass factory.

Early glasses were either fashioned from molten glass collected on a core or poured into a mould, and ribbed bowls or beakers with scenes in relief of gladiators or chariot races made in moulds are a favourite type of the first century A.D. (*80a,b*). The art of blowing glass was discovered in the first century B.C. probably in Syria, and it led to large scale production of much cheaper vessels. From the early manufacturing centres in Syria and Alexandria there was a gradual spread into Italy and the Aegean. As the blowing technique developed, factories making both blown and moulded glass arose in Aquileia and in the Pô valley, and their products reached Switzerland and Austria. The Aquileian craftsmen included a woman, Sentia Secunda, and two green two-handled jugs bearing her name have been found at Linz.

By the early-first century A.D. glass factories existed at Cologne, and by the second century they had sprung up in Belgium and northern France. Meanwhile the Syrian and Egyptian factories continued to flourish, and a number of workers seem to have travelled from east to west so that there was a constant interchange of ideas. The tombstone of one craftsman, Julius Alexander, a citizen of Carthage, has been found at Lyons.

The green jugs with one or two handles became the favourite vessels for second-century cremations (*80c*). More slender wine-jugs of blue, green or colourless glass with spiral ribbing also appear, and vessels decorated with fine coloured threads. Purple or green wine flasks resembling bunches of grapes were probably made in Belgium (*80d*). Facet-cutting, gilding, painting and incised designs were all favourite forms of decoration. Fourth-century pieces include bowls engraved with hunting scenes (*80f*), and the *diatreta* or cage-cups (*80e*) for which the glass was ground down from the outside until the design stood out as openwork. One example from Cologne has a green cage with a band and collar of amber colour, and red lettering inviting the owner to 'Drink and live well for ever'.

80   Glass. a,
b, *design from green
glass cup,
Colchester.* c, *green
glass bottle,
Tongres.* d, *wine
flask, Heerlen.* e,
diatreta, Cologne. f,
*bowl incised with
sun god and
chariots, Cologne*

MONEY

A graffito found in Austria records that the price of a samian
bowl from a mould of Cinnamus of Lezoux was 20 *asses*(*79h*). The
as was a small bronze coin rated at 16 for a silver *denarius*. The
sestertius often mentioned in bequests was valued at four to a
denarius. The rare gold *aureus* was worth 25 *denarii*.

One of Rome's achievements was a coinage of great interest
and variety, acceptable all over the Empire. On one side
appeared the head of the reigning emperor, on the other some
design reflecting the achievements of his reign. Abstract figures of

Peace or Justice, buildings such as the Colosseum or the port at Ostia, various temples, and devices representing the provinces all appear. At a time when no newspapers or radio existed the frequently changed coin types were an excellent means of propaganda.

Banking, money-lending and various credit operations were an essential part of commercial life. Banks were already known in Greece and the Near East in pre-Roman times, and the bankers who extended their activities to the Roman West were largely Greeks. Temples like the shrine of Diana at Ephesus were used as sacred safe-deposits by private persons, merchants and city treasurers, and such funds were lent, initially for mortgages on property. Municipal revenues might also be used as public banks, controlled by city officials and used for loans to meet taxation or lent or invested in various enterprises.

The *nummularii* or money-changers not only exchanged coins of different values and types, they also tested them and picked out forgeries. Forgers found the manufacture of plated coins which imitated silver profitable, and copies were not infrequent. A striking illustration on one of the Neumagen reliefs probably depicts the discovery of a forgery, its owner expostulating to a clerk or bailiff, who regards him with icy disbelief, while several other individuals crowd round to see the offending coin. Inscriptions mentioning *nummularii* are known from Arles, Trier, Cologne and Merida. A Pannonian tombstone shows one seated with his ledger and a bag of money; in front of him a slave is unrolling a scroll, perhaps checking an account.

Interest on loans varied according to the degree of risk incurred. Waxed tablets from the Dacian gold mines record a money-lending partnership between Cassius Frontinus and Julius Alexander on 28 March 167, Frontinus investing 267 denarii and Alexander 500, the profits to be divided. Five years before J. Alexander lent 60 denarii to Alexander, son of Cariccus, to be repaid on demand at the rate of 1 per cent per month. Such a rate was not unusual, other loans to finance shipping might cost more. Part of a mid second-century Egyptian papyrus suggests a transaction which is more in the nature of insurance: the loan is hypothetical and no actual money passes unless disaster over-takes the ship and its cargo, when the agreed amount will be paid to the ship-owner; in return, the high premium of 33 per cent is accepted.

8

Religion and burial

To most of the inhabitants of the Roman Empire the divine force was everywhere, in trees, in streams, in the country and in the sea. From inscriptions, official documents, literature and art there is abundant evidence for the major part the gods played in everyday life, but it is also incomplete evidence and much of its contemporary significance inevitably eludes us. By the first century A.D. various theories concerning the origin of the world had developed in the provinces. The Romans, meanwhile, had acquired many religious ideas from the Greeks and the diverse effects of contacts between the Graeco-Roman cults and the native gods of Syria, Africa, Spain or Gaul etc. give us some insight into the religious attitudes of the time.

ROMAN GODS

As religious considerations permeated Roman society so deeply, it was felt that all important matters were divinely activated and that different gods had charge of particular functions, some of them with overlapping spheres of activity. Jupiter Optimus Maximus, the Best and Greatest, the Roman form of Zeus, was the chief of the gods and regarded by the Romans as their especial protector. Juno was his consort, and Minerva, Mars, Venus, Apollo, Diana, and Mercury were other major deities, as well as Vesta, the goddess of the hearth, Vulcan the smith, and many others of lesser importance. The worshipper venerated whichever gods he felt most likely to fulfil his needs and he judged by results. No moral obligations were involved, success not sin was the vital consideration, but there was also a real anxiety to establish communication. This could be attempted through prayer, sacrifice and divination. In addition to individual prayer, the first two were carried out by the temple priests or by the head of a household in his own home, the third method required specialists.

PRAYERS

The object of prayer was to attract a god's attention and the success of a worshipper's request depended upon the use of the correct forms. Most surviving prayers are in general terms for the health and prosperity of the petitioner, 'me, my house and my household'. The use of such a formula was very strict. If mistakes were made the prayer would be useless and have to be repeated correctly. The most interesting prayers to survive include curses, inscribed on a sheet of lead and nailed up in a shrine. A Spanish example from Turobriga was addressed to Proserpina Ataecina, the goddess of the underworld: 'I beg, pray and beseech you by your majesty to revenge the theft that has been committed against me and to [punish with a terrible death] whoever has borrowed, stolen or made away with the articles listed below: six tunics, two cloaks. . . .' Another example found in the amphitheatre at Carnuntum is also addressed by Eudemus to the underworld powers, here Dispater, Eracina and Cerberus, and to the *larvae*, the ghosts of the amphitheatre dead; again theft seems to be the offence and the curse is inscribed in both Latin and Greek with various magical signs. Elsewhere maledictions were also called down upon fellow competitors and upon those who alienated a sweetheart's affections.

A Roman home usually had a *lararium*, often a cupboard constructed in the form of a model temple, where the household gods resided. The Lares, perhaps the spirits of the land on which the earliest farms were built, became the guardian spirits of the family. A statuette of a dancing boy holding a cornucopia in one hand and a *patera* in the other represented the Lar. The Penates, who watched over the larder and the storehouse, would also be remembered. During meals the head of the house would pour a libation in their honour and pray for their protection. A piece of salt cake would be thrown on to the fire in Vesta's honour. On special occasions there would be more elaborate offerings. When a prayer for some particular favour was made, the worshipper might make a contract, promising that if the petition was granted a special sacrifice or an altar would be offered. Such vows were written on wax tablets tied to the knee of an image of the god. How many prayers were successful is shown by the numbers of altars dedicated with the formula that the supplicant willingly paid his vow.

SACRIFICIAL OFFERINGS

A sacrifice had to have the principle of life to sustain and renew
the vitality of the gods. Cereals made into cakes, flour and salt,
honey, fruit, wine, cheese or milk were the most usual, with birds
or animals for special occasions. Black animals belonged to the
gods of the underworld, otherwise white were chosen, perfect
specimens, garlanded and with gilded horns. The ox for Jupiter,
a horse for Mars, a sheep for Juno – the worshipper could find out
from the temple what was the appropriate offering.

Outside the temple might be a stone altar on which a good fire
was lit. The worshipper said his prayer and with his family and
friends watched the priests and his assistants sacrifice the animal,
to an accompaniment of pipe music played to drown any sounds
of ill omen. A votive relief from Djemila depicts the bronze *patera*,
its handle ending in a ram's head, which was used for pouring
libations, the sacrificial knife and a man stunning a bull; next to
him is a flaming altar, and below a cock and a ram (*81*). The animal
was cut up, the internal organs were examined for any traces of
disease and then burned in the fire, and the rest of the meat was
cooked and eaten. On important occasions an official called a
haruspex would examine the liver for abnormalities, and a model
liver of bronze found at Piacenza marked into various areas
proves that it required skilled study to see whether a sacrifice was
acceptable. An altar at Bath dedicated to the goddess Sulis by
Lucius Memor, *haruspex*, shows this custom was practised outside
Italy. Inscriptions mention others from Aquincum, Virunum,
and Lepcis Magna.

81   Votive relief, Djemila

THE IMPERIAL CULT

With the growth of the Empire a new factor became important in Roman religion: the development of the imperial cult. Before his death Julius Caesar had laid claim to divine honours. Augustus, his successor, inherited a country wearied and ruined with civil war. He made the revival of the worship of the gods and the restoration of the temples a primary concern. As peace and prosperity grew during his reign it is not surprising that he was regarded as superhuman.

In the east rulers had long been worshipped as gods, but not in Italy or in Western Europe. However, as the upsurge of popular feeling grew, a cult of qualified divinity by which offerings were made to the *Genius* or *Numen Augusti*, the divine will or life-force present in Augustus, developed, as part of both public and private observances. Eventually it formed part of the cult of the Lares so that families prayed for the imperial welfare at the same time as for their own. As the imperial cult spread it became clear that it could be a powerful unifying force throughout the Empire. At first permission for altars and temples outside Italy was granted so long as the dedications were to Roma, the goddess of the city of Rome, and to Augustus, with the goddess very much the senior partner. Originally the city goddess, she developed into *Roma Aeterna*, the focus for the emotional loyalty of the Empire's inhabitants(*82a*). The first temple may have been at Alexandria. Others followed elsewhere and in Spain an altar was put up at Tarragona between 26 and 16 B.C. Another altar soon followed at Merida.

The best attested altar to Roma and Augustus, however, is the one at Lyons dedicated by Drusus in 12 B.C. It stood not in the colony but on ground belonging to the sanctuary of the Segusiavi between the confluence of the rivers Rhône and Saône. Strabo describes how it bore the names of the 60 tribes who sent representatives to the provincial assembly which met here, and elected Gaius Julius Vercondaridubnus, an Aeduan who had received the Roman citizenship, as the first high priest. The altar was approached by a processional way lined with statues of priests and tribal dignitaries. On a coin from the Lyons mint it appears decorated with wreaths of oak or laurel with globes on tripods, symbols of Rome's power(*82a*). On either side were columns of local stone, which must have towered above the altar. Hadrian later replaced them with Egyptian syenite, and his

82   Coins. a, *of Tiberius, Altar of Roma and Augustus at Lyons.* b, *of Faustina II,
Cybele.* c, *of Hadrian. Hercules Gaditanus*

columns, cut in half, now support the cupola of the church of St
Martin d'Ainay. On each column stood a winged victory
flourishing a wreath. Bronze letters survive from the altar's
inscription, *Romae et Augusto.*

A few years later another altar with the same dedication was
put up in the territory of the Ubii, the pro-Roman tribe who
occupied the *oppidum* on the future site of the colony at Cologne.
This became the centre for the provincial cult of *Germania.* The
imperial cult also developed in the major cities, often reflecting
local interests such as gratitude to particular emperors.

PUBLIC WORSHIP

As a rule public worship was performed not by professional priests
but by those most actively engaged in public affairs such as con-
suls, governors or magistrates. These priesthoods were eagerly
sought after and might be a very important honour in a man's
public career. In Rome 16 pontiffs, headed by the *pontifex
maximus* (after 12 B.C. this was always the emperor) prescribed the
rites and adjudicated problems of ritual. Also important in Rome
and many other cities were the flamens, each a priest of a
particular cult, chief among them were the priests of the imperial
cult, Jupiter and Mars. Goddesses also had their priestesses

known as *flaminicae*, sometimes, but not always, the wives of the flamens. When a new city was founded a major consideration was the identification of its patron deity, the ordering of its religious calendar and the choice of its priesthoods. Many official rites were carried out by magistrates by virtue of their office. Difficult public prayers were recited by an experienced priest with the magistrate repeating them after him.

Flamens serving the imperial cult in cities were elected by the *ordo*. The office carried certain privileges and the flamens were among the best agents for spreading Romanization. The provincial assembly elected the flamen or high priest of the province from among the tribal delegates, men of the leading families who had already held municipal honours. When their year of office was completed they often went on to important posts outside their homelands. Spain is fortunate in possessing many inscriptions concerned with flamens of the imperial cult. One from Tarraconensis, called Voconius Romanus, was born at Saguntum, educated in Rome, and became a close friend of the younger Pliny who describes him as a delightful companion. He finished up as a Roman senator. When Romanus eventually returned to Spain, Pliny continued to write to him, congratulating him on a new seaside villa and sharing with him concern for a poor grape harvest.

Q. Trebellius Maximus, a flamen of Toulouse, later became chief priest of the provincial assembly at Narbonne. He then went to Athens where he was made a priest of the ancient Athenian cult of Eucleia and Eunomia. The bases of three statues of him have been found in Athens, and the Greek inscription on one found in the Agora records a letter from the magistrates and people of Toulouse thanking the Athenians for the honours bestowed on their compatriot; the Narbonne assembly also wrote to the same effect. Apparently he too could have become a Roman senator, but he refused the offer because he yearned for tranquillity.

With the deification of the empresses, priestesses were also necessary for the imperial cult. They too were elected by the provincial assembly. The office carried great prestige but also certain restrictions on dress and behaviour. A portrait of a *flaminica* appears on a funerary relief from Nîmes(*83*). Licinia Flavilla was the wife of Sextus Adgenius Macrinus, tribune of the Sixth Legion, a magistrate described as a priest (*pontifex*) but not

83   Tombstone. Licinia Flavilla, a flaminica from Nîmes

a flamen. Trebellius Maximus's wife was *flaminica* at Toulouse and seems to have continued there, presumably with another flamen, when her husband went to Narbonne.

In addition to the flamens the imperial cult was served by the college of *seviri augustales*, mentioned on more than a hundred inscriptions in Spain alone, especially from Tarragona and Barcelona. Usually six in number, this was an office primarily intended for well-to-do freedmen, to whom priesthoods were not open. The *seviri* put up dedications to the emperor's *numen* and the deified emperors, sometimes allied with other deities. A *sevir* was regarded socially as an honorary magistrate and in return he would pay for the privilege with the usual public benefactions.

After Tiberius, the imperial cult continued with varying fortunes, reaching its greatest popularity during the peaceful years of Antonine rule. However, from the third century onwards it began to decline as struggles for the imperial power and attacks from outside the Empire suggested that the emperors' *numen* was no longer as powerful. The social prestige of the flamen however, was still attracting the ambitious even when Christianity had become acceptable. The Christian council at Grenada in 309 directed that a Christian flamen who sacrificed to the imperial cult should be excommunicated but one who had merely presided at the games could be reconciled at the moment of death. Flamens who were merely catechumens could be admitted to communion after three years' probation following their period of office.

THE CAPITOLINE TRIAD

The cult of the Capitoline triad also developed in many cities including the colonies although somewhat diminished by the growth of the imperial cult. A relief from Xanten dated 1 July 239, shows the trio standing in a small temple. The usual dedication to Jupiter Optimus Maximus, Juno Regina and Minerva is by a standard bearer of the Thirtieth Legion,

84   *The Capitol, Dougga*

189

stationed at Xanten, for himself and his family. Minerva on the left rests her hand on her shield on which perches her owl. Jupiter in the middle has an eagle by his right foot and grasps a thunderbolt. Juno is accompanied by her peacock. All three hold sceptres.

Capitoline temples are usually found in the forum of a city, as at Xanten, and sometimes in their own precinct at one end of the forum as at Augst(6,7). The Augst Capitolium is a typical classical Roman temple standing on a high podium and approached up steps. The roofed area or *cella* where the statues of the gods resided is not large and is surrounded by an open portico. At the foot of the steps stands a large altar used for the sacrifices and here the priests and other worshippers would gather. A fine example of a Capitol survives in Tunisia at Dougga(84). Here three separate niches were provided, one for each member of the Capitoline triad. Roman temples are always too small for congregational worship. Only the priests and perhaps individual worshippers would enter them.

JUPITER COLUMNS

In the provinces the worship of Jupiter could take other forms. In the Rhine-Moselle region and in north-east and central Gaul tall columns supported a figure of the god. Fragments of one erected in honour of Nero have been found at Mainz. It was put up by two brothers, Q. Julius Priscus and Q. Julius Auctus on behalf of the inhabitants of the settlement outside the legionary fortress. The rectangular base was decorated with reliefs of Fortuna and Minerva, Hercules, Jupiter, and Mercury with his Gaulish consort Rosmerta. Above came a smaller block with the dedication on one side and Castor, Pollux and Apollo on the others. More deities including Neptune, Diana and Epona appear on the drums of the cylindrical shaft which is crowned with a Corinthian capital. The sculptors, Samus and Severus, the sons of Venicarus, probably came from south Gaul. Only a thunderbolt survives from the bronze statue placed on top which is believed to have been a standing figure of Jupiter.

The great period for the Jupiter column however, seems to be at the end of the second and the early third centuries. The majority of them are surmounted by an armed rider who is riding down a giant who supports the horse's front legs on his shoulders as at Epinal(85). Many ideas lie behind this including veneration

85 *Jupiter Column, Épinal*

86 *Jupiter Column, Bonn*

of a successful warrior, and the soldier riding down his enemies which is also a favourite subject for funerary reliefs. Earthly battles, however, are not necessarily involved. The giant probably denotes chaos, darkness and death overcome by the god of life and light. The Celts are known to have venerated sacred trees so the column would appeal to them. Some columns have scale decoration carrying further the idea of the tree, particularly a group of smaller examples found in the Rhineland (*86*). Instead of the rider and giant these are surmounted by Jupiter sitting on a throne, holding a sceptre and thunderbolt. Sometimes a wheel is carved on the side of the throne, the symbol representing the Celtic sky god, Taranis.

MOTHER GODDESSES

Among the deities who decorated the column at Mainz there is one of particular interest, Epona, the great goddess of horses and all concerned with them who was much revered by the Gauls. She usually appears riding side-saddle(*87*), sometimes with a foal following her, or else enthroned among horses. From Gaul her cult spread to Spain, Germany, the Danubian provinces and Bulgaria, many of her altars being dedicated by Gallic cavalrymen. The Romans seems to have adopted her as she is among a number of their deities propitiated by a centurion on the Antonine frontier in Scotland, and she appears in a wall-painting at Pompeii. In some cases she also seems to be associated with springs, or, like Nehalennia, she is a form of mother-goddess.

The mother-goddesses were, of course, a widespread cult originating in the distant past, and crossing provincial boundaries. They had a firm hold on popular affections and offerings to them vary from small clay figurines often nursing one or two infants to the dedications of homesick soldiers remembering the mothers of the homeland. A relief from Vertault showing three of them has already been mentioned (*23* p. 74). Under Bonn Minster evidence for a temple dedicated to the mothers worshipped by the Ubii, the *Matrones Aufaniae*, has been found with numerous fine reliefs. Fig. *89* shows the three women, holding baskets of fruit. In the centre is a young girl, but the other two are older and both wear the large bonnets which were popular with Ubian ladies (p. 108). The relief was dedicated by Q. Vettius Severus a quaestor from the colony at Cologne, in 164. Behind the couch the heads of three worshippers appear. Another relief put up by a Cologne decurion shows a sacrifice in progress(*88*). The priest is veiled with a fold of his toga as he throws incense on to the altar flame from a box held by an attendant, other attendants are bringing the wine jug and *patera* for a libation; on the sides of the altar are girls with offerings of fruit and a youth bringing a piglet which presumably ends up in the cauldron which is being tended over a log-fire(*90*).

MERCURY

It is interesting that some local cults including the mother-goddesses and such variants as Nehalennia do not seem to have been allied with Roman counterparts. This is especially remarkable in the case of Epona with her wide distribution. With increasing Romanization, however, many local deities did become identified with imported Roman gods. Caesar claimed that Mercury was the god most worshipped in Gaul and Lucan in

*87   Bronze statuette of Epona, Loisir,
Jura*

*88   Altar depicting a sacrifice to the
Matrones Aufaniae, Bonn*

89   Relief of the Matrones Aufaniae, Bonn

90   Two details from the sides of 88

the *Pharsalia* mentions the Gallic gods, Taranis, Teutates and Esus as equated with Jupiter, Mercury and Mars. An ancient note on a manuscript of his poem records that Teutates was appeased by suffocating human victims in a cauldron of water. Head-hunting and the veneration of heads and the burning to death of war prisoners were other forms of sacrifice repressed by the Romans. Probably the votive heads found on sacred sites replaced these earlier customs. The appearance of figures carved in wood shows a change in Celtic religious feeling. Before this there was a prejudice against setting up images of the gods. Now, through early Roman or even Greek influences, it seems such figures were made, and with full Romanization they became plentiful.

The study of deities and their names from reliefs and inscriptions shows that a number of local gods might be allied with one Roman one, emphasizing different aspects of his powers. Mercury as a result gains considerably in status in his roles not only as the divine messenger but also as the god of commerce or of arts and crafts. From the big pottery centre at Lezoux comes a statue inscribed *Mercurio et Augusto sacrum*, a

bearded, thick-set peasant, wearing a hooded *byrrus* but with
Mercury's winged hat and a well-filled purse (*91a*). With him are
a cock and a goat, the usual companions of the Gallic Mercury.
On the back of the statue a Celtic inscription tells us that
Apronius made this in honour of Esus, so here Esus is equated
with Mercury rather than Mars.

Several of Mercury's temples are known, often placed on
hilltops. At Berthouville near Bernay a temple at Canetonum
dating from the early first century was destroyed by raiders in 276
but later rebuilt. The temple treasure was buried, and lost until
1830. It consists of 69 pieces of silver, domestic plate dedicated by
worshippers during the whole of that period. One large silver
plate bears an inscription to Mercury at Canetonum, another
shows Mercury with his purse and herald's staff entwined with a
snake (the *caduceus*) in a rural shrine, accompanied by a goat,
cock and tortoise. Julia Sibylla made this offering in the first or
second century.

91   Deities. a, *Mercury, Lezoux.* b, *Serapis, Carthage.* c, *Diana, Ephesus.* d, *Isis,
Cyzicus.* e, *Saturn, Timgad*

MARS

Mars too was popular over a wide range of activities. He was revered not only as a war god but also as Mars Loucetius, the god of light, among the Sequani, and as Mars Teutates, a Celtic god with a name which seems to mean 'god of the people'. Between Trier and Coblenz he is Lenus Mars, an important god of healing with a fine temple near Trier on a sanctuary site of pre-Roman origin. This temple was built in the second century, destroyed in 275, rebuilt, and finally burned under Theodosius(*92*). Here he was also known as Mars Iovantucarus, the friend of the young, and numerous statuettes of children were among his offerings. He shared the site with mother-goddesses known as the Xulsigiae, and round one wall of his precinct was a row of small shrines where country people worshippéd the genius of each rural district or *pagus*. Nearby was a theatre for religious pageants and gatherings.

Provision for the worship of more than one deity at a sanctuary is a common practice; no doubt each cult hoped to profit from pilgrims to the others. In Trier itself a sacred area was found in the Altbachtal with more than 50 shrines closely packed together. Many of them are of Romano-Celtic type, occasionally round or polygonal, but usually square and surrounded by a portico on all four sides giving a characteristic plan of two concentric squares. There was a temple of this type at Pesch (Eifel) in an enclosure which also had an open-air shrine, perhaps with a Jupiter column, and a temple of another type with no

92   Reconstruction. The Temple of Mars Lenus, Trier

93   Reconstruction of temples, etc. Pesch

portico(*93*). Such temples are found in the Celtic provinces with the heaviest concentrations in south-east Britain, in the area around the Seine and Moselle, and in Switzerland, with a few in Raetia, Noricum, and in Pannonia where an example has been identified at Aquincum. None are known in Spain.

NORTH AFRICAN CULTS

In the second millenium the Phoenician explorers set out from the coasts of Syria and the Lebanon, reached North Africa and southern Spain and settled there. Their gods absorbed the local cults and were still a powerful force in the Punic cities during the Roman period. Before Romanization, temple building was unknown, worship being carried on in caves and sanctuaries open to the sky and often on hilltops. These Punic beliefs were austere and cruel, and Baal-Hammon, their chief god, and his consort Tanit-Pene-Baal, demanded human sacrifice(*94 a,b*).

After the Roman conquest of 146 B.C. human sacrifice was forbidden, but the custom persisted in secret, and a governor in the time of Tiberius crucified priests found guilty of it. However, human sacrifice was gradually replaced by offerings of birds and animals, as well as olives, grapes, pomegranates, incense and perfume. Priests were probably celibate and divided into several grades. Some priesthoods may have been hereditary among the leading families.

At home in Phoenicia the cults of Baal and Tanit were not always so important although these gods may sometimes have been worshipped under other names. In North Africa they flourished. There Baal Hammon, 'lord of the perfumed altars', was the chief god of fertility and of the underworld. In the Roman period he was sometimes worshipped as Jupiter, but

94   Deities. a, *Tanit.* b, *Baal Hammon.* c, *Caelestis.* d, *Atargatis.* e, *Aglibol.*
f, *Jarhibol.* g, *Baal Shaman*

more often he survives as Saturn when he appears on votive
reliefs holding a sickle, with one hand to his ear, the better to hear
his worshippers(*91e*). Tanit-Pene-Baal or 'Face of Baal' seems to
represent the great mother-goddess of the Mediterranean and
gradually she tended to grow more important than Baal. In the
Roman period she became Juno Caelestis(*94c*). Caelestis emphasizes her aspect as a sky goddess also connected with Cybele,
the Anatolian form of the mother-goddess.

198

Temples in North Africa

In Tunisia a Punic settlement at Dougga was succeeded by a Roman town which became a *municipium* under Septimius Severus and a colony towards the middle of the third century. Besides the Capitol (*84*) there were more temples near the public baths dedicated to Concordia, Frugifer (the Punic Pluto) and Liber Pater (Dionysus) by A. Gabinius Datus and his son Bassus between 128 and 133. The temple of Concord, here the protective deity of the city, was reached by seven steps from a small court entered through a porch flanked by two columns of red-veined marble. This marble is also used for colonnades which surround the large court of Liber Pater. At one end are five small shrines side by side, the largest one in the centre presumably belonging to Liber and the others to Frugifer and other gods. A dedication to Neptune was also found. At the opposite end of the court is a small theatre.

On the outskirts of the city are more temples, one dedicated to Saturn and the welfare of the Emperor Septimius Severus and his wife Julia Domna, and another probably dedicated to Caelestis. It is placed in the centre of a semi-circular court with a substantial enclosing wall and entrances on either side. A portico with its roof supported by marble columns ran round the curved area and fragments of an inscription found here record that A. Gabinius Rufus Felix gave the land for the temple on becoming a flamen, and the building was completed with legacies from other members of the same family. A silver statue of Caelestis costing 30,000 sesterces is recorded. Statues or busts representing provinces and cities including Dalmatia, Judaea, Mesopotamia, Syria, Carthage, Laodicea and Dougga itself decorated the portico. These are all places devoted to the worship of Caelestis which had received favours from the Severi. The semi-circular court is unique and must reflect Caelestis's importance as a moon goddess.

So in Africa a strong local bias is reflected in the development of religious buildings with shrines set side by side at one end of a large court. A variation of this is a number of small temples each in its own court grouped together as at Thinissut where they seem to be mostly dedicated to Tanit. The triple *cellae*, found repeatedly at Dougga, and known also from Timgad and Djemila, are another favourite African fashion showing a liking for triads, either different aspects of one god, or for different gods as in the Capitol. Temples in the Roman tradition, placed on *podia* and usually found near town centres, vary in size. Some are remarkable for the height of their *podia* as at Djemila where the temple of the Severan family stands at the top of three flights of steps. Another temple with the same dedication dominates the Severan forum at Lepcis Magna. It was approached up a three-sided staircase and had columns with red granite shafts. Some of the porch columns had bases with scenes in relief showing the battles of gods and giants. Inside, the *cella* had a green marble floor.

SPANISH CULTS

In Spain the Phoenician cults also prospered. Most of the Iberian gods they found there seem to have been very local and undeveloped while only a few Celtic deities such as Epona penetrated across the Pyrenees in the north.

One native god, however, does seem to have been of importance: Endovellicus. Like Baal, he was lord of the high places in the mountains north of Seville and his cult extended into Lusitania. One of his sanctuaries has been found near Ebora. More than 50 inscriptions were recovered with fragments of statues and reliefs which had accumulated near the altar. Some were later used for building a Christian church on the site. Coins show Endovellicus was worshipped until nearly the end of the Roman period, but his cult continued to be celebrated in the open air with no evidence for a temple.

At Cadiz the Phoenician Melkart, perhaps identified with some local god, had a famous shrine founded with the city in about 1100 B.C. Here human victims were burnt alive at his festivals. Probably by the beginning of the fifth century B.C. the Graeco-Roman Heracles or Hercules formed one aspect of the cult. After his travels and labours Hercules might be expected to sympathize with a sea-faring and trading community. There are several literary allusions to the temple of Hercules Gaditanus but no precise descriptions: it appears to have included a large court with an altar and shrines, a tower seems to have been a landmark and great doors depicted the Labours of Hercules, perhaps as bronze reliefs. The site was filled with rich offerings and was robbed several times. There is supposed to have been no cult image but a statue appears on coins of Trajan and Hadrian with the legend *Hercules Gaditanus* (*82c*).

This sanctuary is supposed to have been founded as the result of a dream, and it possessed one of the best known oracles which answered problems in this way. Hannibal consulted it and Julius Caesar, after viewing there with envy a statue of Alexander the Great, suffered a nightmare in which he dreamed that he had raped his mother. The Gaditanian priests calmed him with an interpretation that the dream meant he would conquer the world. In A.D. 400, when Cadiz was in ruins, the temple ceremonies were still being carried on.

THE BALKAN AND DANUBIAN PROVINCES

In contrast to Spain, in the Danubian and Balkan provinces of the Empire one finds a mixture of native cults of largely local importance. Some Celtic deities were brought down the Danube by the army, and Greek and Roman gods and oriental cults were spread by traders and the army from Syria and Asia Minor. Temples of the imperial cult and other Roman gods have also been found in Dacia. Apollo and Aesculapius were popular. In Moesia, Silvanus is found along the Danube, and Mars in the east. Nemesis is also important. A mysterious cult very popular in the Danube area is the Thracian Horseman: he appears riding astride, often at full gallop, hunting with a dog, boar or lion. His name and origin are unknown; possibly he combines a protective local deity with an ancient Greek hero cult and an eastern sun god.

CYBELE AND ATTIS

Asia Minor was the home of several important cults which later spread to Italy and the western provinces. The great mother goddess of Anatolia was Cybele, also known as Ma or Magna Mater. Her powers were wide as she was the goddess of fertility, healing, and of wild nature symbolized by the lions which often accompanied her (*82b*). Her young lover Attis suffered castration, death and resurrection, and so symbolized the seasons, with spring following the long, hard, Anatolian winter. As the cult matured it was influenced by Greek philosophy and developed mysteries with various degrees of initiation and ecstasy. The spring festival began on 15 March with sacrifices for the crops, and was followed by a week of fasting and purification. On 25 March banquets celebrated Attis's resurrection. The next day Cybele's image was brought out, bathed and pelted with flowers.

Magnificent processions with richly clad priests and musicians were a feature of this cult which also had a violent side with wild dances and self-inflicted mutilation.

Another feature which developed was the taurobolium in which bulls were sacrificed so that worshippers in a pit below were sprinkled with blood symbolizing their rebirth to a new life. Cybele and Attis were also associated with death, perhaps as a reunion with Earth, and as astral and cosmic powers with an after-life in celestial regions. The moon god Men was sometimes confused with Attis by the Romans but was originally a different deity with an important sanctuary at Antioch in Pisidia. He was also a healing god and a giver of oracles.

TEMPLE ESTATES

Such temples were supported by large temple estates, an important feature of pre-Roman Asia Minor which continued into the Roman period, and Cybele and Men were among the greatest landowners. At Comana in Cappadocia, the priest of Cybele at Ma was master of 6,000 temple servants who lived in a settlement near the temple, supported by revenues obtained from the neighbouring countryside. Gradually the temple estates tended to be absorbed by developing cities and they lost much of their power and wealth under the Romans.

On a hillside at Ephesus was the ancient shrine of a local goddess, later combined with the Greek Artemis and the Roman Diana, the guardian of wild animals who hunted by moonlight attended by her nymphs. Statues show her wearing a garment probably of leather, decorated with eggs, bees, rams, lions, oxen and griffins(*91c*). Croesus's name occurs on columns from an early temple destroyed in 356 B.C. This was rebuilt by Alexander the Great and became one of the 'Wonders of the World'. The Goths burned it down in A.D. 273. Among the rich gifts received by the temple were 31 gold and silver statuettes of Diana given by C. Vibius Salutaris in A.D. 104.

From early times the goddess owned extensive estates in the Cayster valley including quarries, pastures, fishing rights and salt-pans. Like many temples in Asia Minor this one had long possessed the right of sanctuary. Under the *Pax Romana* it was no longer needed for political refugees from the wars of the Hellenistic kings. The area had grown unreasonably large and the privilege was abused by criminals and other dubious characters. Under Augustus the Asian cities were requested to send delegates to Rome to establish the rights of temples to offer sanctuary, and these rights were somewhat curtailed.

TEMPLES IN ASIA MINOR

The first building in Ephesus to be dedicated to an emperor was the Temple of Domitian in the city centre opposite the agora. Little of it survives apart from an altar and part of a colossal cult statue, but its existence entitled the city to the title of 'Temple Warden of the Emperor'. This became Twice Temple Warden when a temple was erected to Hadrian by P. Quintilius. The fragments of this building have been re-erected and 95 shows the porch with an arch over the entrance adorned with a bust of the city goddess. The relief visible inside the porch dates from a fourth-century restoration and shows the Emperor Theodosius and his family on either side of Diana of the Ephesians; at each end of the row of 13 figures is Minerva with spear and shield. It seems that even a Christian emperor still had to respect the city goddess.

Diana's twin brother Apollo had several important temples in Asia to which worshippers came to consult oracles. At Claros, near Notion, not far from Ephesus, there was a holy place in a wood by a sacred spring mentioned by Homer. A Hellenistic temple was approached by a processional way lined by statues. The oracle was always consulted at night when the priest entered

95   Temple
of Hadrian,
Ephesus

a room beneath the temple and drank from the spring. The prophecies were delivered in verse. Inscriptions at Claros, many of them of the second century A.D., record delegates from eastern Europe and Thrace arriving with problems, and the oracle's replies are recorded from as far afield as southern Russia, Dalmatia, Algeria and Rome itself.

THE SYRIAN DEITIES

In Syria we meet at home some of the deities which the Phoenicians took to Africa. Baal, the lord, occurs not infrequently in the Old Testament and while the Baals of different cities may differ slightly in character, it appears that powers over victory, sun and rain, fertility and the future life were all combined in this one god. Unlike the Greeks and Romans, the Syrians made little attempt to apportion responsibilities between different deities. A professional priesthood supervised punctilious and complicated ritual and magnificent processions with lavish sacrifices, including human victims in pre-Roman times.

The chief deities in north Syria were the Mesopotamian pair Baal-Hadad and his consort Atargatis (*94d*). Atargatis, a giver of fruitfulness, developed associations with the moon and with the planet Venus. At her cult centre at Hierapolis on the Euphrates, according to Lucian, her statue had a turreted crown with a great ruby and her robes were adorned with jewels; in her hands she held a sceptre and a spindle. Fish seem to have been sacred to her and a fish-pond at Hierapolis was dedicated to her. The fish answered to their names, the chief fish having a gold ornament on his fin. Beside Atagartis's statue sat a golden statue of Hadad with a long pointed beard holding a spèar and a flower. Simia or Simios completed a triad which became Romanized as Jupiter, Venus and Mercury. The same triad is found at Baalbek (Heliopolis) and here Jupiter Heliopolitanus seems to be an amalgam of Baal-Hadad with the Sun-God.

Syrian temples

The temple at Heliopolis was reached up a flight of steps leading through an entrance into an hexagonal forecourt and then into a larger court surrounded by porticos. Red Egyptian granite from Assuan, grey Bosphorus granite and probably imported marbles were used for the columns. Two altars existed in the court, the larger one was 16·6 m. (53 ft) high. Two staircases led to

96   *The temples, Baalbek*

the top. Both altars were flat-roofed and were probably artificial high places where the sacrifices were performed. Two pools in the courtyard provided water for ritual purposes. The altars date back to the first century as does the temple of Jupiter, built of the local honey-grey limestone. Six columns nearly 20 m. (65 ft) high still stand on the podium to show its unusual height and size (*96* on left). Above the columns was a frieze of bulls' and lions' heads, the animals of Hadad and Atargatis.

Outside the court and beside the temple of Jupiter another temple was added in the second century (*96*, foreground). Commonly attributed to Bacchus, the identity of its owner remains uncertain. Unusually well-preserved, its elaborate decoration survives in the coffered ceiling of the north side of the portico, decorated with figures of Mars, Victory, Diana, Vulcan, Bacchus, Ceres and other deities. The interior was reached through a monumental doorway surrounded by a beautiful and intricate carving of foliage in which appear cupids, birds, fauns, small animals, bunches of grapes and garlands. Inside was a double row of niches originally occupied by statues. Steps lead up to a raised sanctuary with a crypt beneath. This type of sanctuary is really the throne-room of a god rather than the simple *cella* of a Greek deity and his priest, and seems to represent the survival of native Semitic traditions. Several small Lebanese temples such as Temple A at Niha show it well, and it also occurs at Gerasa (Israel) and Petra (Syria).

In eastern Syria at the great centre of the caravan trade, Palmyra, reigned a triad of local deities. Bel is equated with Jupiter and also known as Baal Shamin, and with him appear Jarhibôl and Aglibôl, representing the sun and the moon (*94e-g*). An inscription mentions the dedications of Bel's temple and this building dates from the first century A.D. At first sight it looks like a conventional Roman temple except that the entrance is in the centre of one of the long sides. The roof, however, is partly flat and terraced, perhaps it is an artificial high place, reached by interior staircases. Inside two shrines at the top of flights of steps face each other across the length of the building. Other deities worshipped at Palmyra include the caravan gods Arsa and Oziza.

CROSS-FERTILIZATION

In the west Romanization in the first two centuries A.D. tended to transform the native cults, although the Phoenician importations into Spain and Africa proved more resistant. In the east, however, many of the ancient sanctuaries maintained their rites and ceremonies, probably in their native tongues. The Roman influence was far slighter, even when lip-service was paid by adding Jupiter or Hercules to the original names. Not content with local prestige many of the gods crossed the seas and gained adherents in the west. This missionary work was done by the army, slaves and traders.

Roman religion, as we have seen, was a punctilious, well-ordered affair, offering limited opportunities for individual devotions. Aelius Aristides indeed found in Aesculapius a god on whom he could rely for guidance in his way of life, and probably the healing and some of the mystery cults came nearest to fulfilling the need for a more intimate relationship. Oriental cults often had a stronger appeal either through their colourful services and processions with music and dancing in honour of such deities as Cybele or by their moral challenge to lead a better life as with Mithras (see p. 209). Such religions taught their worshippers how to free the soul from the tyranny of the body and of suffering, to attain a state of ecstasy, to be born into a new life on earth and to hope for a blessed immortality after death. Gods such as Attis or the Egyptian Osiris died and were extravagantly mourned by their consorts, Cybele or Isis, and their followers. When they were resurrected their rebirth into a new life was rapturously celebrated. Frequent services and sacred repasts maintained interest so that the worshipper's senses, his intellect and his conscience might all be involved.

THE SPREAD OF ORIENTAL CULTS

It is not surprising that Cybele with her background as a mother-goddess found adherents as far afield as Gaul and probably Britain, especially as she was firmly established in Rome itself. In 205 B.C. the Sibylline books had warned the Romans that Hannibal could only be finally defeated if they enlisted the aid of the Great Mother. So in the guise of a sacred black aerolith from the temple at Pessinus she duly arrived in Rome and was established in the temple of Victory with satisfactory results. However, Attis and the more colourful features of her worship which came with her shocked the Romans, and the cult continued in a subdued form until Claudius encouraged it as a rival to that of Isis which had been introduced into Rome by his predecessor Caligula. Inscriptions and statues of Cybele and Attis are known in many provinces, and temples probably existed at Lyons and Vienne. Writers such as St Augustine mention the processions, and as late as the sixth century Gregory of Tours describes the goddess's carriage being drawn by oxen through the fields and vineyards at Autun.

ISIS AND SERAPIS

Syrian cults also spread to the west, frequently as a result of troop movements. Jupiter Dolichenus, the god of war and iron, and so perhaps originally a Hittite deity from Doliche in Commagene, was one army favourite. Others include Jupiter Heliopolitanus and Malakbel. Traders, on the other hand, were largely responsible for carrying the gentler Egyptian cults of Isis and Serapis all over the Empire, sometimes together, more often separately.

Isis was the queen of heaven and earth, life and death. When Osiris, her consort, was killed by Set, she searched for his body, eventually finding it at Byblos, a Phoenician port on the Syrian coast. There she restored it to life, and, as in the cult of Cybele, festivals and ceremonies recalled these incidents annually. Serapis was originally the god of Memphis and became merged with Osiris as a god of healing and the underworld. He also could be a god of fertility wearing a grain measure as a crown(*91b*), a sun god, a form of Dionysus, or even Jupiter. The legend can also be regarded as an allegory in which Isis represents the Egyptian plains fertilized annually by the Nile floods (Osiris), but at other seasons kept apart by the desert (Set).

In the Roman period Isis tended to become the predominant partner(*91d*). She was a favourite with the women of Spain, one of whom, Fabia Fabiana, dedicated an altar to her for her granddaughter Avita, probably a priestess, at Guadix (Acci) near Grenada. This records the gift of 37 kilos of silver which was made into a diadem, earrings, a collar, rings and bracelets decorated with jewels including pearls, emeralds, a jacinth and a carbuncle. Even ornaments for sandals were included, all presumably for a statue. Apuleius is known to have been a devotee of Isis and the imposing remains of one of her temples have been found at Sabratha.

Serapis also had a temple at Sabratha and another one at Lepcis where statues of him with Cerberus, the many-headed underworld dog, were found, and also one of Isis. Another important temple of Serapis has been discovered at Ephesus. Statues and inscriptions confirm the existence of temples to both deities in the western provinces and the Danube area, and priests and priestesses are also mentioned.

The rituals used in the Egyptian cults were far older than those of the other religions of the period, being based on texts engraved on monuments of the earliest Pharoahs. The daily round began with the uncovering of the statue at dawn, the lighting of the sacred fire and the pouring of water. The statue was dressed and adorned with jewels and silently adored by initiates during the day. Then another service accompanied the covering of the statue and the closing of the sanctuary for the night. All this went on with musical accompaniment. Isis appealed particularly to women, and originally looked kindly on all their activities, even including prostitution which was also sometimes a feature of the cult of Cybele. By the second century, however, she had become more straitlaced and favoured illicit love no longer. Similarly the priest's ritual ablutions grew into ceremonies of purification which could wipe out sin. The sensual element of the cult diminished and the initiate strove for purity and right living in order to avoid retribution in the after-life.

MITHRAISM

The last and best known of the oriental cults which spread over the Roman Empire is that of Mithras. It probably came from Persia where the sky god Ahura Mazda was venerated with lesser deities, particularly Mithras, the pure genius of light. Persian immigrant invaders brought the cult to Asia Minor in pre-Roman times via Mesopotamia, and in the Semite cults Ahura Mazda became Bel, and Mithras became Shamash, the sun god. Because the Persians were hereditary enemies of the Greeks the cult made little progress in the eastern world. According to Plutarch, the Romans became acquainted with it when fighting some pirates in Cilicia. From Italy in the late first century it gradually spread into the west.

The mythology of this cult relates how, in the distant past, Mithras was miraculously born out of a rock, cared for by shepherds and had various adventures. One such adventure was some form of combat with the sun god, which resulted in an alliance between them so close that the two are sometimes identified as one, with the title *Sol Invictus Mithras*. Mithras also hunted down and sacrificed a mysterious bull and from this sacrifice came blood which was a sign of life and the seeds of various useful plants; this was Mithras as the creator bringing new life to the world. A relief showing the bull-slaying was usually placed in the Mithraea, which were caves, real or artificial, divided into a nave with aisles lined with benches on which the worshippers reclined. Mithras is often accompanied by his dog, and statues of Cautes and Cautopates, figures representing the rising and setting sun.

Initiates worked their way through seven grades from the Raven through the Bride, Soldier, Lion, Persian and Courier of the Sun, to the Father. Converts passed through a preparatory novitiate, were vowed to secrecy, and subjected to severe ordeals of heat and cold, probably in a drugged state. The cult was confined to men only and many of the initiates were soldiers. Truth, justice and loyalty, especially to fellow initiates, were expected of Mithras's followers. Belief in evil as personified by Ahriman, the god of darkness, as well as in the powers of light, brought a new factor into Roman religion: the Mithraist saw life as a continual struggle between good and evil. Mithraea, temples to Mithras, were never large, but their numbers increased rapidly. Rome is said to have had more than a hundred. The discipline and high ideals of Mithraism appealed to many although some may have lacked the courage to attempt initiation.

Three Mithraea have been found at Carnuntum. The oldest was constructed under Vespasian by men of the Fifteenth Legion which included Asiatic recruits. This was restored in the third century but long before this the temple was too small and another was built next to a shrine of Jupiter Dolichenus. Early in the second century, when the town was developing, a third and larger Mithraeum was needed(97). The reconstruction shows a lion and a stoup for holy water at the entrance, and the torch-bearers Cautes and Cautopates standing by the pillars which separate the aisles. The Mithraeum was reached down a stairway through a large entrance hall. It was enlarged at the beginning of the fourth century. Diocletian met his fellow emperors there and they dedicated an altar to the god.

Germany, so long a battlefield, is the richest province for Mithraic finds with a notable group of reliefs illustrating the god's adventures. Three temples have been found at Heddernheim, and evidence for others is known from the frontier and from Augst, Strasbourg, Mainz and Cologne. Five have so far been identified in Britain. A typical relief comes from Karlsruhe (Neuenheim) where the centrepiece shows Mithras killing the bull(98). The act gives him no pleasure and he turns his head away at the crucial moment; Cautes and Cautopates are on either side of him, busts of the sun and moon are in the top

97   *Reconstruction of mithraeum, Carnuntum*

98 Mithraic relief, Karlsruhe

corners, and above both appear driving their chariots. The main theme is framed by a number of smaller scenes with, on the left, Mithras's birth from the rock and his pact with the sun-god, and on the right, the catching of the bull and its transport to the cave. The cult reached its peak at the end of the third century when the Emperor Diocletian was initiated; had Christianity not intervened, the whole Empire might have succumbed to Mithras.

BELIEF IN AN AFTER-LIFE

Roman beliefs concerned with life after death developed gradually and remain to us rather nebulous. Virgil echoes earlier Greek beliefs with a picture of the soul descending to a world of dim spirits, including the unburied dead, past a hell where some evil-doers suffer fantastic tortures. Then, in Charon's boat, the rivers and marshes which lead to the happy sunlit world of the Elysian fields are crossed. The idea that the individual survived as a person still concerned with those left on earth continued to develop during the Empire, especially among those initiated into the mystery cults of Mithras and Dionysus, among others. With it, as we have seen, grew the conviction that a good life would be rewarded in the hereafter.

The grave was the earthly home of the dead, revisited by them at certain times. These included birthdays and other anniversaries, and Roman public festivals such as the Parentalia from 13 to 21 February when temples were closed and no marriages celebrated, attention being focused on the dead. Groups of relatives with flowers and milk and wine for libations visited the family tombs. At the end of the period there would be a family gathering. On 9, 11, and 13 May came the Lemuria when the ghosts connected with a household returned to haunt it, not all with very kindly intentions. Various rites were necessary to repel them. The ancestral ghosts were also remembered when the daily offerings were made to the Lares and Penates.

BURIAL CUSTOMS

Burials vary in elaboration from the simple cremation with the ashes buried in a glass or pottery vessel to elaborate tombs resembling miniature houses. Tombs might contain a single occupant or a number of cremations or coffins. Grave goods similarly vary in scale from a single pot to everything a wealthy man might need in the after-life. At Weiden near Cologne a large underground vault is lined with niches intended for cremations. Three larger spaces are faced with pieces of marble so that they resemble couches, and on them were placed the busts of a man, a woman and a girl. The vault was reached down steps and sealed with a heavy stone door which slid up and down in grooves, balanced by weights. Inside are two full-scale basket chairs modelled in stone, perhaps for the mourners on ceremonial occasions. Later a fine sarcophagus was placed in an upper chamber. Too heavy for the floor, it eventually subsided into the room below (*99*).

Another unusual burial comes from Simpelveld (Holland) where the remains of an early third-century lady were buried with her gold necklace and ear and finger rings. The interior of her coffin is carved with reliefs depicting some of her possessions including the baths of her villa. She herself can be seen lying on a couch. A başket chair, a three-legged table, cupboards, a chest, toilet articles, and a low table for glass and metal vessels also appear. Many coffins have decorated exteriors but the Simpelveld example with its pictures intended purely for the re-assurance of the departed is unique. Was it perhaps carved under her supervision before she died? Such care for the final resting place is typical of the period, and well shown by a second-century will from Langres. The name is lost but the anonymous testator mentions a chapel already constructed, and directs that his statue be erected in a room outside it and his ashes be placed in a fine marble altar. An inscription was to record his name and age and the names of the contemporary magistrates. Stone couches and

99   Burial chamber, Weiden, near Cologne

benches with coverlets, pillows and woollen robes were to be
provided for the members of the family and some of the freedmen
and freedwomen when they came to offer sacrifices six times a
year. If his heir, Sextus Julius Aquila, a nephew, aided by the
bailiff and others, failed to carry out the will's instructions, the
city of Langres could demand a fine of 100,000 sesterces. All
sporting equipment, bath utensils, medicines, embroideries, his
litter and his sedan chair were to be cremated with the dead man.

Coffins

Burial in coffins tends to replace cremation from the second
century onwards although examples of skeleton burials occur in
some areas as a continuance of pre-Roman customs as early as the
first century. Coffins were of wood or stone, sometimes with plain
lead inner linings.

Examples survive of fine carved stone sarcophagi intended to
either stand above ground or, more frequently, to be placed in a
tomb. They form a series developing from the early second to
the sixth centuries, many of their decorative features proving
suitable for Christian as well as pagan burials. Two main groups

are distinguishable, the western or 'Roman', and the eastern or 'Greek'. The Weiden sarcophagus is an example of a Roman type carved on the front and on the rounded ends, but with the back left plain to stand against a wall(*99*). Its scenes of seasons and cupids are also typical. Decorative scenes from elsewhere include Dionysiac revels, hunts, battles, voyages to the Isles of the Blessed, and scenes of daily life. Sarcophagi with garlands slung from the shoulders of cupids or nymphs were another favourite, the garlands representing those offered to the dead.

The eastern type illustrates the extensive trade in marble for architectural decoration and funerary monuments which had developed between Greece and Asia Minor and the rest of the Empire. They were normally carved on all four sides. The Attic sarcophagi of Greek marble occur not only in Greece as far north as Salonika, but were also exported to Cyrenaica, Thrace, Bithynia, Italy, southern Gaul and Spain in the second and third centuries. Lids representing gabled roofs or sculpture showing the deceased reclining on a couch, accompanied them.

A second eastern group, the Asiatic sarcophagi, came from Asia Minor. Quarries at Docimium and Aphrodisias may have supplied much of the marble. They were numerous in Asia Minor, but most of the exports went to Italy. Their symbolism as the abode of the dead was emphasized with a door carved on one of the ends. One example from Side shows a fine double door partly ajar with a dog looking out(*100a*); winged victories decorate the angles. Another from a woman's burial shows a fan leaning against the door between a spindle and a basket of wool(*100b*); a butterfly and a swallow flying by denote mourning

100 a,b. *Coffin reliefs from Side*

214

for the soul on its journey to the next world. The name has been erased and replaced by that of Ctetus Dionysius; presumably he re-used the coffin.

As much of the sculptured detail on the sarcophagi was so delicate, they were usually blocked out and transported in an unfinished state, sometimes with a piece left attached for the lid. A Roman wreck found near Taranto had a cargo of coffins possibly of marble from Aphrodisias; some were double units, others nested one inside another. They date from the first half of the third century. Greek and Asiatic craftsmen and sculptors followed such cargoes and completed the work to the customer's specifications in Rome and other centres. At Lepcis Magna a dedication to Aesculapius was put up by Asclepiades, *marmorarius* from Nicodemia.

Marking the grave

Above ground the whereabouts of burials were indicated by wooden markers or tombstones. In general the sanctity of a grave was respected but the decay of the marker might cause the burial to be disturbed. Some grave-diggers, indeed, seem to have worried little about existing burials, and examples are known where, on land difficult to dig, earlier remains were ignored to avoid the extra exertion needed to cut fresh graves. The importance of tombstones to historians as a source of information for the nationality, age and rank of the deceased has already been stressed, likewise the value of funerary reliefs for information about clothing, crafts etc.

Barrows, circular mounds of earth marking the site of rich burials, occur in some areas along the Danube, in Thrace, and round Trier. They continue a tradition well-known in prehistoric times. In Italy, meanwhile, circular tombs of masonry, largely inspired by the Etruscans, developed under the Empire. It is believed that with the spread of Romanization such tombs influenced native traditions still surviving among the well-to-do provincials, and resulted in some splendid burials in the late first and second centuries. This fashion was adopted with particular enthusiasm in Belgium where evidence for 350 examples has been found. They range from 1 to 10 m. (3–33 ft) high, steep, conical mounds usually covering a single cremation placed in a pit lined with planks or stones a few feet below ground level. Fig. *101* illustrates a fine group from Omal, surmounted by trees.

101   Row of barrows, Omal

A recent Belgian excavation of a barrow at Berlingen in the Hesbaye uncovered a cremation with the ashes of a young man placed in a large glass bowl interred in a timber-lined vault. Eight small ritual pits held the remains of the funeral banquet. There were also nine glass vessels, two lamps, iron tools and the head of a hunting spear. Three samian plates were all made by the potter Felix and so was a larger dish with two handles. Seven small samian cups and several coarse pottery wine flagons ensured that thirst would not trouble the dead man(*102*). All the samian came from the southern Gaulish potteries and gives a date of between A.D. 70–80 for the burial. A small protective mound may have been first piled over it and then a barrow 28 m. (92 ft) in diameter was constructed. A number of simpler second-century cremations found nearby seem to be more in accord with prehistoric traditions and belong to poorer folk. The barrow's inmate probably lived at the villa which was found 375 m. (1,230 ft) to the south.

At Tirlemont (Brabant) a woman's cremation placed in a lead coffin was found in 1951 with a trinket box, bone hairpins, a coin of Trajan, and bronze fluted bowls fitting into each other and used as a bain-marie for keeping food hot. Another barrow at Tirlemont produced the bronze jug and *patera* used for pouring libations which have often been found. Rarer items from other rich Belgian barrows include a bronze lantern from Herstal, Liège, a glass flask imitating a bunch of grapes from Frésin (Limbourg) and a lizard of rock-crystal from Cortil-Noirmont. Britain, too, had well-furnished barrow burials, probably the result of Belgian contacts. A stronger Italian influence is

102   Barrow interior, Berlingen

probably reflected by the fine stone-built structure under a
barrow at Antoing-Billemont, Hainaut. The local Tournai
quarries provided the large blocks for its circular retaining wall,
covered passageway, and two chambers. It was robbed in 1654.
Like the Weiden tomb it could be entered to deposit fresh burials.

Pillars and tower tombs

Pillars and towers which must often have made familiar
landmarks, were also provincial favourites. In north-east Gaul
the rich merchants put up rectangular pillars several storeys high
decorated with portraits, and scenes of daily life or of religious
significance. Reliefs from fragments of such monuments at Arlon
and Neumagen have already been mentioned (p. 53). At Igel, 3·5
km. (2 miles) outside Trier, one monument 23 m. (75 ft) high still
stands, from the early third century(*103*). Rich textile merchants, Secundinius Aventinus and Secundinius Securus, erected
it in honour of their dead parents. Originally brightly painted,
the central scene shows two men with a youth between them;
more members of the family appear on the other sides with
pictures of domestic and business activities above and below.

   Tower-tombs, masonry structures several storeys high with
architectural ornamentation of various kinds, are particularly

217

103   Funerary column, Igel

important in North Africa and the east Mediterranean. At Palmyra they date from the mid-first century B.C. to the third century A.D., increasing in size so that more burials could be added. Tripolitania has both obelisks and temple tombs. Away from the coast cemeteries of people made wealthy by the African caravan trade survive at Ghirza. Traces of their large fortified farms occupied in the third and fourth centuries also remain. Fig. *104* shows one side of a temple-tomb built on a platform decorated with a scroll pattern using grapes and pomegranates. The burial chamber lies beneath the tomb. Columns support an arcade with scenes of hunting and agriculture. In the dedication

104   Tomb. Ghirza

Nimmire and [M]accurasan pray that their parents Chullam and Varnychsin may visit their children and grandchildren.

Architectural ornament is featured still more strongly in the tombs cut out of rock faces round Jerusalem and at Petra. These show a combination of Semitic burial customs and Graeco-Roman influences. Arabia became a Roman province in A.D. 106, and in the second century six tombs were constructed with façades cut out in relief. The earliest is the Khazne. Its second storey has a charming circular pavilion in the centre with a square structure on either side; these have friezes of flowers, fruit, and masks. A figure of Abundantia holding a cornucopia stands in the pavilion and Amazons decorate the square features. Inside the lower

219

storey steps lead into a vestibule. The main burial chamber lies through a richly decorated doorway.

Cemeteries

Cemeteries lined the approaches to Roman cities. Outside Tyre (Lebanon) numerous graves have been excavated on either side of the road leading to the Roman arch erected in the second century(*105*). The sarcophagi are mostly of Proconnesian marble and some of them were re-used in the Byzantine period. Land for graves could be purchased from municipalities, imperial estates or private owners. Space in large tombs or small family cemeteries was also sometimes sold. A Cologne tombstone put up to the freedman M. Petronius Albanus, aged 30, carefully records the area of his grave as 5·4 m. (18 ft) square.

Hygiene and the sanctity of the grave enforced burial outside towns and the Urso charter forbids the construction of new crematoria within half-a-mile of the city with a fine of 5,000 sesterces for any infringement. The body on its bier was burnt either on the site of its eventual burial or in special cremation areas. One was identified at Carmona near Seville where a cemetery containing more than 900 burials, mostly cremations was found. Some were placed in underground tombs reached by steps, with room for a number of urns accompanied by pottery, glass or metal grave goods. One tomb contained a painting of the dead feasting. Others had banqueting arrangements for mourners with masonry couches. The Tomb of the Elephant had three

105   Cemetery. Tyre

dining-rooms, one with a garden open to the sky; a kitchen was also provided.

Gardens associated with tombs have been found in many western provinces and several were incorporated in a walled cemetery outside Salona. The Greek-speaking eastern provinces also indulged in them and a number existed outside Alexandria. A second- or third-century Alexandrian inscription mentions such a garden dedicated to Pomponia Mousa by her son and husband. It was to be held in common by their family and their freedmen and freedwomen for ever. Later it was claimed, probably by a descendant of the freedmen, that the garden and the tomb had been sold illegally and this accusation seems to have been substantiated in court and damages awarded. The sale of the grapes, flowers, and vegetables grown in such gardens helped towards the upkeep of the tomb and its ceremonies.

LIFE EXPECTANCY

Much remains to be learnt from the study of burials. Roman cemeteries used during at least three centuries have been found round such towns as Cologne and Tongres, and seven major ones have been identified at Amiens. A detailed examination of the grave goods found with such abundant material can throw light on local manufactures and trading contacts, while inhumations may show traces of disease.

The expectancy of life of the peoples of the Empire is still debatable and varied according to climate and social conditions. Here inscriptions, of course, assist the student. We know that infant mortality was heavy, and that death in childbirth was a serious danger. In the second half of the second century the Marcomannic wars brought the plague to Noricum where it was rampant for some time. A tombstone records how one family was wiped out by it in the year 182 while the apparent closure of several cemeteries in the province about this time may reflect depopulation. A study of tombstones at Dougga, however, shows an unusual proportion of people of advanced age, 10 per cent being over 90, 5 per cent reaching 100, and one surviving to the age of 115. In general, however, people were not optimistic about their prospects of living to see their children reach maturity and still less their grandchildren. This accounts for the stress laid on the importance of the family and the need to cherish the memory of the dead.

9

Conclusion

This work has touched briefly on a number of topics in an attempt to summarize various aspects of Roman provincial life, especially the more unfamiliar. It deals with a period when it was possible to travel freely over a wide area of Europe, western Asia and North Africa, needing no passport, speaking one widely-understood language, and using one generally acceptable currency. As we have seen, these conditions greatly assisted the interchange of ideas and beliefs as well as of material objects.

Faced with so much information of varying value one can only regret the inevitable omissions. If, however, this book reflects some of the fascination of its subject and perhaps stimulates further study, it will have served its purpose.

Appendix 1

Chronology of Roman Emperors

23 B.C.	Augustus
A.D. 14	Tiberius
37	Gaius (Caligula)
41	Claudius
54	Nero
68–9	Galba
69	Otho, Vitellius
69	Vespasian
79	Titus
81	Domitian
96	Nerva
97	Trajan
117	Hadrian
138	Antoninus Pius
161–80	Marcus Aurelius
176–92	Commodus
193	Pertinax
193–211	Septimius Severus
198–217	Caracalla
217	Macrinus
218	Elagabalus
222	Severus Alexander
235	Maximin Thrax
238	Gordian I, II, III
244	Philip and others
249	Decius and others
253	Gallienus and others
259–74	*Imperium Galliarum*. Three Gallic usurpers rule Spain, Gaul, Britain and Germany 260–69 Postumus

	269–71	Victorinus
	271–4	Tetricus
268	Claudius II	
269	Aurelian and others	
275	Tacitus	
276	Probus	
282	Carus	
283	Carinus and Numerian	

Empire split into four administrative sections under two Augusti and two Caesars

| 284–305 | Diocletian |
| 286–305 | Maximian |

Britain. Two usurpers rule in Britain and N. Gaul.

	287–93	Carausius
	293–6	Allectus
293–6	Constantius Chlorus. *Retakes Britain 296*	
293–311	Galerius	
305–7	Flavius Severus	
305–13	Maximin Daia	
306–12	Maxentius	
308–24	Licinius	
306–37	Constantine I *Sole Emperor of East and West,* 324	
317–40	Constantine II	
333–50	Constans	
324–61	Constantius II	
350–3	Magnentius	
355–63	Julian	
363–4	Jovian	
364–75	Valentinian I	
364–78	Valens	
367–83	Gratian	
375–92	Valentinian II	
385–8	Maximus	
384–8	Flavius Victor	
392–4	Eugenius	
379–95	Theodosius I	
395–423	Honorius	
395–408	Arcadius	
408–50	Theodosius II	
425–55	Valentinian III	

Appendix 2

Roman Provinces

ACHAEA Southern Greece

AFRICA PROCONSULARIS Eastern Algeria, Tunisia, and western Libya

ARABIA Jordan and western Saudi Arabia to the Red Sea

ARMENIA Between the Black Sea and the Caspian Sea

ASIA Western Turkey

BAETICA Southern Spain

BITHYNIA and PONTUS Northern Turkey along the southern coast of the Black Sea

BRITANNIA England, Wales and Scotland as far north as the Antonine Wall frontier from the Firth of Forth to the Firth of Clyde

CAPPADOCIA Eastern Turkey

CARIA, LYCIA and PAMPHYLIA Southern Turkey

CILICIA South-east Turkey

CYRENAICA Eastern Libya

DACIA Most of Romania

DALMATIA Hungary south of the river Save, most of Yugoslavia and part of Albania

EPIRUS Western Greece

GALATIA Central Turkey

GALLIA AQUITANIA The Atlantic coast and south-west France to the Pyrenees

GALLIA BELGICA France north of the river Seine to the Upper Moselle, most of Belgium

GALLIA LUGDUNENSIS Central France from the Atlantic coast and the river Seine on the north to the river Saône, and from south of the river Loire to Lyons

GALLIA NARBONENSIS Southern France from Lyons to the Mediterranean, from Narbonne to the Alps

GERMANIA INFERIOR Holland, Belgium east of Antwerp, and Germany west of the Rhine as far south as Andernach

GERMANIA SUPERIOR Both sides of the Rhine south of Andernach and east to near Stuttgart. On the west to the south of Strasbourg the province takes in south-east France as far as Langres, and most of Switzerland

HISPANIA TARRACONENSIS North-east Spain from north of the river Douro and the Pyrenees, and east of a line from near Toledo and west of Cartagena to the Mediterranean coast

JUDAEA Israel from north of Caesarea to south of Gaza

LUSITANIA Portugal south of the river Douro

MACEDONIA Southern Albania and northern Greece

MESOPOTAMIA The area between the rivers Tigris and Euphrates bordered by Roman Syria and Armenia

MOESIA From Dalmatia to eastern Romania and the Black Sea, also Bulgaria south of the Danube

NORICUM Austria south of the Danube to the Alps, and east from the river Inn to just short of Vienna

PANNONIA East of Noricum it included Hungary south and west of the Danube as far east as Budapest, and Yugoslavia north of the river Save

RAETIA Bavaria and western Austria, east of Germania Superior to the boundary with Noricum on the river Inn

SYRIA Syria and Lebanon from the eastern Mediterranean coast to the river Euphrates

THRACE Most of Bulgaria south of Moesia including the European coasts of the Black Sea, the Bosphorus and the Sea of Marmora

Bibliography*

GENERAL

ABBOTT, F. F. and JOHNSON, A. C., *Municipal Administration in the Roman Empire*, Princeton University Press, 1926.

BALSDON, J. P. V. D., *Life and Leisure in Ancient Rome*, Bodley Head, 1969.
    Rome. The Story of an Empire, Weidenfeld & Nicholson, 1970.

BIEBER, M., *History of the Greek and Roman Theatre*, Princeton University Press, 1961.

BOETHIUS, A. and WARD-PERKINS, J. B., *Etruscan and Roman Architecture*, Oxford University Press, 1970.

BURFORD, A., *Craftsmen in Greek and Roman Society*, Thames & Hudson, 1972.

BUTLER, A., *Sport in Classic Times*, E. Benn, 1930.

CARCOPINO, J., *Daily Life in Ancient Rome*, Routledge & Kegan Paul, 1956.

CASSON, L., *Ancient Mariners*, V. Gollancz, 1959.

CHARLESWORTH, M. P., *Trade Routes and Commerce into the Roman Empire*, Hutchinson, 1926.

CHEVALLIER, R., *Roman Roads*, Batsford, 1976.

DAVIES, O., *Roman Mines in Europe*, Oxford University Press, 1935.

FLOWER, B. and ROSENBAUM, E., *Apicius: the Roman Cookery Book*, Harrap, 1974.

FORBES, R., *Studies in Ancient Technology*, Brill, Leiden, 1955–63.

FRANK, T. ed., *An Economic Survey of Ancient Rome*, John Hopkins, Baltimore, 1933–40.

GRANT, M., *The Climax of Rome*, Weidenfeld & Nicolson, 1968.
    The World of Rome, Weidenfeld & Nicolson, 1960.

GRIER, J. A., *A History of Pharmacy*, Pharmaceutical Press, 1937.

JONES, A. H. M., *The Cities of the Eastern Roman Provinces*, Oxford University Press, 1937.

* Published in London unless otherwise stated.

LEWIS, N. and REINHOLD, M., *Roman Civilisation. II. The Empire*, Harper Torch Books, New York, 1966.

MARROU, H. I., *A History of Education in Antiquity*, Mentor, New York, 1956.

MILLAR, F., *The Roman Empire and its Neighbours*, Weidenfeld & Nicolson, 1967.

OGILVIE, R. M., *The Romans and their Gods*, Chatto & Windus, 1969.

ROSTOVTZEFF, M., *The Social and Economic History of the Roman Empire*, Clarendon Press, Oxford, 1959.

SINGER, C., HOLMYARD, E. J., HALL, A. R., and WILLIAMS, T. A., *A History of Technology. Volume II*, Clarendon Press, Oxford, 1956.

TOYNBEE, J. M. C., *Animals in Roman Life and Art*, Thames & Hudson, 1973.

    Death and Burial in the Roman World, Thames & Hudson, 1971.

VERMASEREN, M. J., *Mithras, the Secret God*, Chatto & Windus, 1963.

WHITE, K. D., *Roman Farming*, Thames & Hudson, 1970.

WILD, J. P., *Textile Manufacture in the Northern Roman Provinces*, Cambridge University Press, 1970.

AFRICA

BROUGHTON, T. R. S., *The Romanisation of Africa Proconsularis*, John Hopkins, Baltimore, and Oxford University Press, 1929.

CHARLES-PICARD, G., *La Civilisation de l'Afrique Romaine*, Librairie Plon, Paris, 1959.

ÉTIENNE, R., *Le Quartier Nord—Est de Volubilis*, E. de Boccard, Paris, 1960.

HAYNES, D. E., *Antiquities of Tripolitania*, Antiquities Dept. of Tripolitania, Tripoli.

RAVEN, S., *Roman Africa*, Evans, 1969.

REYNOLDS, J. M. and WARD-PERKINS, J. B. ed., *The Inscriptions of Roman Tripolitania*, British School in Rome, London/Rome, 1944.

ASIA

AKURGAL, E., *Ancient Civilisations and Ruins of Turkey*, Mobil Oil Turk A.S., Istanbul, 1970.

BEAN, G., *Aegean Turkey*, E. Benn, 1966.

    Turkey beyond the Maeander, E. Benn, 1971.

    Turkey's Southern Shore, E. Benn, 1968.

MAGIE, D., *Roman Rule in Asia Minor*, Princeton University Press, 1970.

MANSEL, A., *Die Ruinen von Side*, W. de Gruyter, Berlin, 1963.

MILTNER, F., *Ephesos*, Verlag F. Deutcke, Vienna, 1958.

BRITAIN

FRERE, S. S., *Britannia*, Routledge & Kegan Paul, London, 1967.

LIVERSIDGE, J., *Britain in the Roman Empire*, Routledge & Kegan Paul, London, 1968.

RICHMOND, I. A., *Roman Britain*, Penguin, 1963.

TOYNBEE, J. M. C., *Art in Britain under the Romans*, Oxford University Press, 1964.

DACIA

MACKENDRICK, P., *The Dacian Stones Speak*, Funk & Wagnalls, New York, 1975.

DALMATIA

WILKES, J., *Dalmatia*, Routledge & Kegan Paul, 1963.

EGYPT

BELL, H., *Egypt from Alexander the Great to the Arab Conquest*, Oxford University Press, 1948.

WINTER, J. G., *Life and Letters in the Papyri*, Michigan, 1935.

GAUL

AUDIN, A., *Lyon. Miroir de Rone dans les Gaules*, Fayard, Lyons, 1965.

BONNARD, L., *La Navigation intérieure de la Gaule à l'époque Gallo-Romaine*, Universitaires Press, Paris, 1913.

CHADWICK, N. K., *Poetry and Letters in Early Christian Gaul*, Bowes & Bowes, 1955.

DUVAL, P. M., *La vie quotidienne en Gaule pendant la paix Romaine*, Hachette, Paris, 1952.

ÉSPERANDIEU, E., *Recueil géneral des Bas-reliefs, statues et bustes de la Gaule Romaine*, Imprimerie Nationale, Paris, 1907–66.

ÉYDOUX, H.-P., *La France Antique* , Plon, Paris, 1962.

FOUET, G., *La Villa Gallo-Romaine de Montmaurin*, Editions du Centre National de la Recherche Scientifique, Paris, 1969.

HATT, J. J., *Histoire de la Gaule Romaine*, Presses Universitaires de France, Paris, 1959.

La Tombe gallo-romaine, Presses Universitaires de France, Paris, 1959.

WANKENNE, A., *Le Belgique à l'époche romaine*, Centre national de recherches archéologique en Belgique, Brussels, 1972.

WIGHTMAN, E., *Roman Trier and the Treveri*, Hart-Davis, 1969.

GERMANIA

BOGAERS, J., *De Gallo-Romeinse Tempel te Elst*, Staatsdrukkerij en Vitgeverijbedrijf, The Hague, 1955.

ÉSPERANDIEU, E., *Bas-Reliefs de la Germanie romaine*, Les Editions G. van Oest, Paris, 1931.

FREMERSDORF, F., *Das Römergrab in Weiden, bei Köln*, Verlag der Löwe, Cologne, 1957.

HONDIUS-CRONE, A., *The Temple of Nehallenia at Domburg*, J. M. Meulenhoff, Amsterdam, 1955.

LA BAUME, P., *Colonia Agrippinensis*, English translation, Greven Verlag, Cologne, 1967.
    The Romans on the Rhine, English translation, W. Stollfüss Verlag, Bonn.

LAUR-BELART, R., *Augusta Raurica*, Historischen und Antíquarischen Gesellshaft, Basel, 1969.

MACKENDRICK, P., *Romans on the Rhine*, Funk & Wagnalls, New York, 1970.

NORICUM

ALFOLDI, G., *Noricum*, Routledge & Kegan Paul, 1974.

SCHÖBER, A., *Die Römerzeit in Österreich*, R. M. Röhrer, Verlag, Vienna, 1954.

PANNONIA AND MOESIA

GOLLOB, H., *Führer durch Karnuntum*, Sensen Verlag, Vienna, 1960.

MOCSY, A., *Pannonia and Moesia*, Routledge & Kegan Paul, 1974.

OLIVA, P., *Pannonia and the Onset of Crisis in the Roman Empire*, Nakladatelstvi Československé Akademie Ved, Prague, 1962.

SZILAGY, J., *Aquincum*, Verlag des Ungarischen Akademie des Wissenschaften, Budapest, 1956.

SPAIN

ÉTIENNE, R., *Le Culte Imperiale dans la Péninsula Ibérique, d'Auguste à Diocletien*, E. de Boccard, Paris, 1958.

MACKENDRICK, P., *The Iberian Stones Speak*, Funk & Wagnells, New York, 1969.

PIDAL, R., *Historia de España II. España Romana*, Esposa-Calpe S.A., Madrid, 1955.

SUTHERLAND, C. H. V., *The Romans in Spain 217 B.C.–A.D. 117*, Methuen, 1939.

THOUVENOT, R., *Essai sur la Province Romaine de Bétique*, E. de Boccard, Paris, 1940.

WISEMAN, R., *Roman Spain*, Bell, 1956.

SYRIA

CHAMPDOR, A., *L'Acropole de Boalbek*, A. Guillot, Paris, 1959.
Les Ruins de Palmyra, Les Haut Lieux de l'Histoire, Beirut, 1963.

DOWNEY, G., *A History of Antioch in Syria from Seleucus to the Arab Conquest*, Princeton University Press, 1961.

THRACE

WIESNER, J., *Die Thraker*, W. Kohlhammer Verlag, Stuttgart, 1968.

Index

The numbers in bold type refer to the figure numbers of the illustrations.